THE BOXERS
OF WALES

Volume 2: Merthyr
Aberdare & Pontypridd

GARETH JONES

ST DAVID'S PRESS

Cardiff

Published in Wales by St. David's Press, an imprint of
Ashley Drake Publishing Ltd
PO Box 733
Cardiff
CF14 7ZY
www.st-davids-press.com

First Impression – 2011

ISBN 978-1-902719-29-0

British Library Cataloguing-in-Publication Data.
A CIP catalogue for this book is available from the British Library.

CONTENTS

ACKNOWLEDGEMENTS

No book like this is the work of just one person. Most important, of course, there are the boxers, past and present. Without their great deeds, there would be nothing to write about. Those still among us have been ready and willing to recall their exploits; the families and friends of those long gone have been similarly happy to share their memories.

Many others, in and around the sport, have also played their part.

I am indebted to Ken Buchanan for contributing the foreword; to *Boxing News* and its editors past and present, Claude Abrams and Tris Dixon; to the British Boxing Board of Control, represented by general secretary Rob Smith, Lynne Conway and the girls at its Cardiff HQ, and Mark Warner, secretary of the authority's Welsh Area Council; to John Waith, of the Welsh Amateur Boxing Association; and to Don James, Johnny Jones and Wynford Jones, of the Welsh Ex-Boxers' Association.

I am grateful to the friendly staff at Merthyr Borough Council, Cyfarthfa Castle and Pontypridd museums and in the local studies departments of Cardiff Central, Pontypridd and Aberdare libraries, while particularly acknowledging the help and encouragement of the inimitable Carolyn Jacob at Merthyr Library.

There have been many individuals, too, who have lent a hand. They include Bill Donovan, Colin Jehu, Stan Thomas, Dick 'The Drummer' Gibbs, Bill Long, Brian Coleman, Gareth Harris, Matthew Bozeat, Mary Wheeler and a number of family historians on the Rootschat and Rootsweb forums in Wales, England and the US, known to me only by their pseudonyms.

The book's illustrations have mostly been provided by those listed above, but I must also acknowledge the generosity of the professionals who have allowed me to use their work: Huw Evans Picture Agency (www.huwevansimages.com) and Robert Haines (www.roberthaines.com). Thanks go also to Meic Stephens for permission to quote lines from the poetry of the late Leslie Norris.

My enthusiastic publisher, Ashley Drake, also deserves my gratitude.

And, as ever, I pay tribute to the labours of the indefatigable Harold Alderman, MBE, a distant relative of 1920s Pontypridd flyweight Hector. Harold is still collecting and collating old fighters' records at an age when most would be settling for a cup of tea and a crossword. Without his efforts and generosity, authors like myself would find life much more onerous.

FOREWORD

Arriving in Merthyr from a big city like Edinburgh was a bit of a culture shock. I travelled up on the train from Cardiff and we stopped at every little station. It felt like Thomas the Tank Engine. By the time we reached Merthyr, I was desperate to get to the gym and take it out on the bag – and wondering whether I could face that journey again.

But once I got to know the place and its people, it was a different story and I ended up staying for five years. The Welsh have always been fantastic to me and I love them.

Merthyr, in particular, was buzzing. Everybody wanted to talk about boxing. It was the big thing for them when it came to sport.

I remember spending hours in the Station Café, just chatting about fighters. For my manager, Eddie Thomas, it was like his office. People were always ringing there to speak to him. We'd arrive and Tony Viazzani would say, "Eddie, there's been a call from Jack Solomons - can you ring him back?" And Eddie would get on the blower and discuss his business, with the old coffee machine puffing and whistling away in the background.

Some things were a bit surprising. I stayed in Dowlais with some lovely people in Myfanwy and Bryn Jones, and their son, Phil, is still one of my closest friends. But I'll never forget mentioning that I fancied a bath and discovering it meant a tin one in front of the fire!

It was great to have Myfanwy and Phil there when I was made an honorary citizen of Merthyr in 2004. That was one of the proudest nights of my life.

There were always a few old-timers around the gym and I enjoyed meeting the likes of Cuthbert Taylor and Danny Dando, but never really knew what they had achieved. This book fills in the gaps and pays tribute to the great boxers who have come from this marvellous town and its neighbours.

Ken Buchanan, MBE
World Lightweight Champion 1970–72

INTRODUCTION

Is there any other town on the planet which boasts three statues of boxers?

Ever since Merthyr Tydfil began to grow on the back of coal and iron, the hard men those industries employed have used their fists to solve disputes. That, in turn, produced local heroes who would then fight for the entertainment of their colleagues.

Those warriors who swapped punches on the mountainside became "civilised" with the introduction of the Queensberry Rules – the work of a Welshman, John Graham Chambers, although published under the name of his patron, the Marquess - and the increased use of gloves. But the sport lost none of its appeal. Nor did its more orderly nature make it acceptable to those who claimed moral authority over the town.

In 1900 the pastor of Tabernacle was one such critic. "Pugilism is the craze of the time," he lamented. "It has swept over South Wales like a fatal epidemic. It has reached the little schoolchildren, who are heard on the streets discussing the merits and demerits of certain fighters."

It is ironic that 97 years later his chapel was overflowing for the funeral of one of those pugilists, Eddie Thomas.

The fistic tradition in the town was so embedded that James Winstone – good fighting name, that – reacted to defeat in a 1915 parliamentary by-election by challenging his conqueror to a bout. Funny, really, considering that Winstone had stood, in the middle of World War I, as a pacifist.

This book, of course, has extended its reach beyond Merthyr and the neighbouring Cynon Valley to include Pontypridd. Some would say Ponty should be combined with the Rhondda, planned for Volume 3 of this series, but I prefer to think of it as part of the Taff Valley.

Instead, Rhondda gets the man named in 2009 as the greatest British boxer of the previous 100 years. Jimmy Wilde was, it is true, born at Quakers Yard, but he moved as a toddler to Pontygwaith and learned his fighting trade there.

Readers will no doubt come up with others they feel should have been included. Some are name-checked among the Supporting Cast, others have missed out altogether. That should not diminish their place in the area's sporting history. This book is intended as a tribute to them all.

GARETH JONES
Cardiff, February 2011

JERMAINE ASARE
(1983–)

🥊 Commonwealth Games Bronze Medallist 2010

As a youngster, he dreamed of banging in the goals for Cardiff City or their great rivals down the M4.

Asare was born in Cardiff to a Ghanaian father and Jamaican mother, who moved to the Graigwen area of Pontypridd when he was just a toddler. His soccer skills saw him train with the Bluebirds and then have a spell on schoolboy forms with the Swans, but he lost interest in the game and turned his hand to boxing.

Even though he was 17 before the first laced on the gloves, the switch proved a wise decision, a successful career culminating in an unexpected spot on the podium at the 2010 Commonwealth Games in Delhi.

Asare soon discovered he had a talent for his new sport, but suffered a setback when his local gym opted to focus on training rather then competitive boxing. Jermaine headed up the valley to the Merthyr Ex-Servicemen's club, with Gareth Donovan taking over his tuition.

Early attempts at the Welsh ABA championship foundered – twice at the hands of useful Anglo-Welshman Rhys Davies, now an unbeaten pro – but he kept at it and was rewarded

Jermaine Asare

with the title in 2010, his three wins topped off with a final points success over North Walian Kia Joinson at Swansea's revamped leisure centre.

Appearances in the Welsh international vest suggested that the selectors had their collective eye on the young electrician and he was duly picked as one of the eight-strong team for India. Once there, as the pre-Games medal tips crashed out, the unsung Ponty boy just kept on going.

Although the luck of the draw condemned him to a prelim outing where most of his rivals had byes, it proved no problem as he used his 6ft 1in height and long arms to outpoint Tarieta Ruata, from the Pacific archipelago of Kiribati. Ghanaian Olympian Ahmed Saraku proved a tougher proposition and Jermaine only scraped through on countback in a low-scoring bout, but he improved on a slow start in the quarter-final to take a 10-4 verdict over Samoan Filimaua Hala.

That was as good as it got. Lincoln-based Scot Callum Johnson, who had already shocked English hope Obed Mbwakongo, proved just too good, establishing a substantial lead before the referee stepped in to rescue the exhausted Welshman.

A disappointing ending, but, for someone whose ambition on arrival was "just to win one bout", a bronze medal is more than adequate consolation. Asare now plans to give the pro game a try.

CHARLIE CHEW
(1903–1968)

🥊 Welsh Featherweight Challenger 1929

The son of a confectionary salesman – presumably known as Chew the Sweets! – Charlie grew up in East Avenue, in the Gadlys area of Aberdare, but was living in North London by the time he emerged as a player on the national boxing stage.

Despite being based in Hendon, Chew still appeared regularly in his native land and made sufficient impression to be matched with Rhondda-born Ginger Jones in an official eliminator for the Welsh feather crown. Their meeting in Bridgend ended all-square, but it was Charlie who was given the shot at the vacant title, facing another Rhondda boy, Billy Evans, in Merthyr on March 16, 1929.

The Ystrad boxer brought skill to the occasion, Chew aggression. The more subtle approach won the day, with Billy more than clever enough to evade Charlie's charging attacks. And it was not just defensively that Evans was superior: he landed frequently enough to cut his Aberdare foe over the right eye, before a right hook split open an already swollen left ear, leaving both men drenched with blood.

Evans was clearly superior and there was no dissent when his arm was raised at the end.

Charlie Chew

Two months later Chew headed west to Llanelli and a rematch with Ammanford-based Jones, who this time emerged with the 15-round points verdict. Ginger went on to dethrone Evans and reign for a couple of years over Wales's nine-stoners.

Chew, on the other hand, turned his back on his homeland and focussed on earning a crust on the lively London scene. He was twice outpointed by future British champion and world title challenger Seaman Tommy Watson and had multiple meetings with other decent practitioners, such as Moe Moss, Sid Raiteri and Dick Stubbings.

After hanging up the gloves, Charlie stayed in his adopted home, marrying there and raising a family, while passing on his knowledge to young hopefuls at the Ex-Servicemen's Club on West Hendon Broadway, known locally as 'The Madhouse'. He is remembered there as "a quiet man, stocky, with cauliflower ears".

REDMOND COLEMAN
(1872–1927)

🥊 Welsh Flyweight Claimant

The Iron Man From Iron Lane is unlikely to have a statue erected alongside Merthyr's later champions. After all, he was hardly a role model. But his place in the town's fistic history is secure, even if most of his punches were thrown without official sanction.

How many fights he had, between the ropes or on the mountain, will never be known. Most were never reported, certainly not in the respectable pages of the *Merthyr Express*. But that publication did record that a court appearance in 1922 was the 127th time he had appeared before the beak.

Coleman earned his nickname from his birthplace in Georgetown, the second child of Irish labourer John and his Merthyr-born wife, Ann. His real name, according to the note of his baptism in the parish register of St Mary's RC Church, was Raymond Henry Coleman, though that may have been the mistake of a deaf priest.

Despite his fearsome reputation, he was no taller than 5ft 6in, and as a teenager was accepting challenges at a mere seven stone. He soon began to style himself the 7st 12lb champion of Wales, but when he knocked out Pontypridd's Daniel Evans at Merthyr Drill Hall in 1892, the match was made at 8st 4lb.

Promoter Patsy Perkins took Coleman to London for a couple of trial bouts in which he made a good impression, but he disliked the big city and headed home. It was more than a year later, in April 1894, that he had the chance to

Redmond Coleman, 'Emperor of China'

display his skills before the toffs of the National Sporting Club – Resolven giant Dai St John boxed there the same evening – and duly demolished Bristol's Curley Howard inside a round. Howard, who had already suffered a broken arm in the brief encounter, struck his head on the boards when floored and had to be treated at Charing Cross Hospital.

The first known loss on Redmond's sketchy record came at the hands of local Ross Mazey when Perkins's booth was based in Swansea. The Merthyr man was down twice in the ninth and it ended two sessions later.

There were numerous clashes with fellow-townsman Jack Murphy, including two in four days at the Prince of Wales Circus, each ending inconclusively when Murphy was struck by cramp after seeming in control.

The Coleman legend, however, had little to do with these gloved battles, more his fights on the cobbles. On one occasion he was taking a hiding from a much heavier visitor to Merthyr when there was a cry of "Come on, Redmond!" Suddenly realising who he was taking on, the stranger promptly fled!

He once fought hated rival Tommy Lyons on the site of the Ynysfach coke ovens, a popular spot for score-settling; apparently the fight was prompted by a case of Chinese whispers, Coleman having discovered a cat eating his dinner. He threw it out accompanied by a demand to "Bring me a **** lion!" By the time the story had spread across town, it had become, "Bring me **** Lyons!"

The author Alexander Cordell paints a picture of Coleman as a handsome figure, surrounded by adoring women. In reality he was described as having the skin of an elephant, his head pocked with dents left by the sister with whom he lived "under the Arches", who used to control him with liberal use of an iron bar. She and the local priest, Father Flood, were said to be the only two people, male or female, he would never strike – and even the clergyman carried a large stick in case he changed his mind.

He certainly had no fear of the police, once flattening two of them and hanging them by their uniforms from chapel railings. The law came out on top frequently enough, however, that century of misdemeanours including brothel-keeping alongside the inevitable drunkenness and affray.

Redmond was still using his fists into middle age, although his run-ins with the authorities apparently dwindled after a lenient stipendiary had urged him to "go away and be a good boy". Yet there was never any doubt where his instincts lay. On his death bed, delirious, he is said to have punched a nurse before finally leaving the arena.

DANNY DANDO
(1904–1983)

✍ Welsh Bantamweight Champion 1929

I f his father had been less of a tyrant, and young Danny had not been so kind-hearted, the lad might never have become a boxer.

It all revolved around the family Christmas cake. Danny had cut off the crusts to give to a hungry friend; Dad was not pleased and threw what was left at his 15-year-old son. The youngster brushed off the stray currants, ran upstairs, hurled some clothes into a case and began walking to join big brother George. It promised to be a long march: George was in Newcastle.

In the Midlands, a kindly policeman took him home for a meal and then gave him the money to complete the journey by train. Not that his brother, by then carving out a career in the ring, was particularly pleased to see him. He took Danny to the gym at Newcastle Orthopaedic Hospital, where he was training some of the doctors, put the gloves on him and finally floored him with a few digs to the stomach. George then told him he was going to fight for a living.

Having learned the basics on Tyneside, Danny returned to South Wales, where, confusingly, he was billed as 'Young Dando', the same name George had used earlier. But people soon knew exactly who he was. The authorities certainly did and on February 2, 1929, he met Cardiff-based Ulsterman Minty Rose at Snow's Pavilion in Merthyr in the climax to a tournament organised by the Welsh Boxing Association and Control Board – the British Board as we now know it was officially formed just nine days later – to find a successor to the late Tosh Powell as Welsh bantamweight champion.

Dando was the cleverer boxer at range, particularly effective with left uppercut, while Rose was too cautious, letting Danny build a lead by halfway. The Belfast boy gradually came into contention, troubling Dando in the ninth and cutting him in the 11th. He maintained his aggression until the end, but Danny's defence was good enough to keep him ahead and earn the verdict, even if the loser disagreed.

Danny Dando

Dick German's Cartoon: The Welsh Bantam Title.

An alternative view of Danny's scrap with Cuthbert Taylor

His reign was brief, however, as he was outpointed less than six months later by cross-town rival Cuthbert Taylor, although the clash took place in Pontypridd. The challenger dominated throughout and although Dando lasted the distance, he was a sorry figure at the end. Hopes of another title shot were dashed when local boy Stan Jehu outscored him in an eliminator at Maesteg.

Like so many of his contemporaries, Danny toured with the fairground booths, where punters could earn £1 if they survived three rounds with him, though he only earned £2 a week himself. He suffered his first knockout when he fooled around, carrying one unlikely looking character around the ring on his shoulders; ordered by his boss to put him down, he was immediately flattened by a blow to the jaw.

Danny and some young admirers at Penydarren ABC

Back in the "proper" game, Dando met George Morgan at Bargoed in an eliminator for a crack at Welsh feather king Ginger Jones. Morgan was often lax in his attitude to training, but on this occasion he was fit and ready. Dando, on the other hand, was below par and was repeatedly beaten to the punch. The defeat was a signal that his career was drawing to its close.

Long after retirement, he began to suffer blackouts and doctors were unable to discover the cause. Danny thought they might be the result of blood from all his fights, which had congealed in his nose, so he stuck a hazel twig up his hooter. There was gore all over the place for a while, but he never had a problem again.

GEORGE DANDO
(1888–1938)

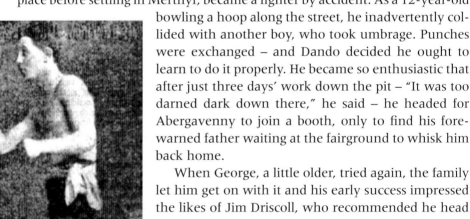 British Flyweight Claimant 1910

The oldest of five boxing brothers was probably known in Wales as much for his feud with Jimmy Wilde as for anything he achieved in the ring. Their families lived at opposite ends of the same block in Pontygwaith and the two boys' rivalry continued when they worked down the same pit – and later they traded blows in two title fights.

Cheshire-born George, the son of a bootmaker who moved from place to place before settling in Merthyr, became a fighter by accident. As a 12-year-old

bowling a hoop along the street, he inadvertently collided with another boy, who took umbrage. Punches were exchanged – and Dando decided he ought to learn to do it properly. He became so enthusiastic that after just three days' work down the pit – "It was too darned dark down there," he said – he headed for Abergavenny to join a booth, only to find his forewarned father waiting at the fairground to whisk him back home.

When George, a little older, tried again, the family let him get on with it and his early success impressed the likes of Jim Driscoll, who recommended he head for the fistic hotbed of Newcastle, and arranged for local sportsman Sammy Cohen to look after him. His route had taken him via Scotland, where he met local star Jim Easton on January 24, 1910, for what was billed as "the English seven-stone title" – the word 'British' was rarely used in those days and the Scots and Welsh just had to accept it – but the 20-round contest ended inconclusively in a draw. It was the nearest George came to a championship.

He married a Geordie lass and soon became a popular figure on Tyneside, where one journalist described him as "a tiny wonder, a fast and fierce

George Dando

George hits the road with Hartlepool promoter Billy Wall

two-fisted fighter, with an old cranium that gives him a big advantage over his opponents". He could "take a bit, too, this Welsh boy" and charmed the public with a lively sense of humour.

With the National Sporting Club introducing weight divisions as we know them, there was much interest when it was announced that Londoners Sid Smith and Joe Wilson were to contest the first flyweight Lonsdale Belt. Dando and another Cockney, Bill Kyne, met at Newcastle's St James's Hall a few days before in a match it was hoped would put the winner next in line. The pair served up a war described as one of the best ever seen at Gallowgate, but Kyne's harder punch saw him edge the verdict – not that he ever had his title shot.

A run of victories saw George matched with Sammy Kellar at Liverpool Stadium on Boxing Day 1912 in what was optimistically billed as a showdown for the world flyweight crown. Few outside Merseyside saw it that way – and Dando was forced to retire after 15 rounds, anyway.

Eight stone was really too heavy for George, who took renewed aim at another mighty midget, his old foe Wilde. Jimmy won a 15-round decision in Tonypandy before the pair met again at the American Skating Rink in Cardiff's Westgate Street on September 22, 1913, for the "Welsh and English" 7st 10lb championship. Dando actually managed to put the elusive Wilde on his backside, but was floored himself by the next punch and needed the bell to save him. He survived the full 20 rounds, but lost the decision.

It was close enough for a rematch three months later, with the same two titles on the line, this time at the Drill Hall in Merthyr. The bad blood was still evident as George was warned for standing on Jimmy's foot to keep him still long enough to hit; when he then landed a solid thump after Wilde had slipped over, the referee turfed him out.

The Welshman served in the Northumberland Fusiliers during World War I and was wounded on the Somme, but recovered to continue his career well into the 1920s. He died at Cowgate, in his adopted city, at the age of 50.

COLIN DAVIES
(1950–)

🥊 Welsh Light-Middleweight Challenger   1974

The ginger-headed youngster from Aberfan followed some mates to Eddie Thomas's Penydarren gym and, as so often happens, the mates dropped out, but he stayed. Three Welsh schoolboy titles proved it was a wise choice.

But then his other sporting talent took over and he began to represent Merthyr Schools at football. The ring took a back seat for six years – until a chance meeting with another red-haired southpaw, former middleweight Johnny Gamble, in town. "I've just opened a gym," said 'The Gambler'. "You should come along."

Colin's return bore fruit with a Welsh ABA championship, prompting him to turn pro with Hughie Thomas, whose brother Eddie used his influence to arrange regular work on the London dinner-boxing circuit.

After a debut win at the World Sporting Club, Davies's unveiling on home turf turned out unhappily when he was stopped on cuts by Llantwit Major's Clive Collins. The gash was on the other eye when they met again, however, the bout being halted in Colin's favour and the Aberfan fighter claimed a points decision in the all-southpaw rubber match, dropping Clive in the first.

He then wrecked the debut of another lefty, Mike Manley, knocking the Monmouthshire man out in five, improving on that with a first-round stoppage in a rematch. The victories were part of a seven-bout winning streak which earned him a shot at the inaugural Welsh light-middle belt.

Colin Davies covers up as Larry Paul moves in

In the opposite corner at the Club Double Diamond, Caerphilly, on March 26, 1974, was another Davies, from the North Walian branch of the clan. Dave Davies headed south with a big reputation. The Bangor bricklayer was an outstanding amateur, striking silver for Wales at the Commonwealth Games in Edinburgh, and had lost only once in his first six outings as a pro in the care of Corwen-born world title challenger Alan Rudkin.

There were high hopes for Dave at the time – though he never fulfilled them after his British title chances were wrecked by future world champion Maurice Hope – and he was a hot favourite. But Colin had the greater skill and controlled the first three sessions, before the Northerner's strength began to have its effect. As he slowed, the welder from Merthyr Vale Colliery became drawn into a head-down tussle. The outcome was inevitable. His right eye closing from the sixth, Colin could not keep Dave away and his brutal body shots dropped the valley boy three times before referee Jim Brimmell rescued him in the eighth.

There was talk of a rematch, but when Colin produced the best performance of his life in flooring and outpointing Merseysider Tim McHugh, a man who had beaten Dave, it was seen by Rudkin, who had another boxer on the card. Soon came the news that Dave could no longer make light-middle and the fight was off. Coincidence? Maybe.

The bout was resurrected at full middleweight, where the Welsh title was also vacant. But when Colin arrived at the Grosvenor House in London's Mayfair he discovered that his namesake had pulled out, claiming injury. Instead he was to face former British champion Larry Paul. Physically fit, but mentally deflated, the Merthyr man was battered to defeat inside five rounds, though he was never off his feet.

Disgusted at the turn of events, Davies walked away from the sport, although he did spend a few years helping trainer Gareth Donovan at the Merthyr Ex-Servicemen's club.

DAI DAVIES
(1983–)

🥊 **Welsh Super-Featherweight Champion   2006–08**

🥊 **Welsh Featherweight Champion   2009–10**

The two novices battling it out beneath the stand at Bristol City's football ground had only three pro fights between them. But their amateur pedigrees were obvious as Dai Davies and Riaz Durgahed served up a superb four-rounder, before the Welshman's arm was raised in triumph.

Durgahed had been good enough to represent his native Mauritius at the Sydney Olympics, while the boy from the Gurnos was a Four Nations junior gold medallist and wore the Welsh vest at numerous international competitions.

Those who saw him take Durgahed to school were sure they had seen a future champion. But, unfortunately, their confidence never seemed totally shared by Davies himself. Despite winning Welsh titles at two weights, Dai will know all too well that he never fulfilled his potential.

He was not helped by some ambitious matchmaking. In his next bout he was put in with a debut-making Martin Lindsay, already seen as an exceptional prospect. The Ulsterman blitzed Dai inside a round. It sparked a run of five straight losses, including revenge for both Durgahed and former amateur victim Derry Mathews and defeats at the hands of Londoner Matthew Marsh and Yorkshireman Gary Sykes. Lindsay, Marsh and Sykes all went on to become British champions.

Yet the talent was still there. Davies dented Jamie McDonnell's 100 per cent record with a draw; McDonnell is now the top man in Europe. He ended the seven-bout winning streak of Turkish-born Devonian Jed Saygi. And on August 8, 2006, Dai collected his first Welsh championship, outpointing ringwise Pembrokeshire traveller Henry Jones in a Sunday afternoon thriller beneath the garish murals of Swansea's Brangwyn Hall.

Victory in a rubber match with Durgahed at Rhydycar reinforced hopes that the Merthyr boy might, after all, make the grade at a higher level. He then lost his next five. They were, as before, against good men: unbeaten prospects Akaash Bhatia and Ricky Owen, three-weight Commonwealth champion

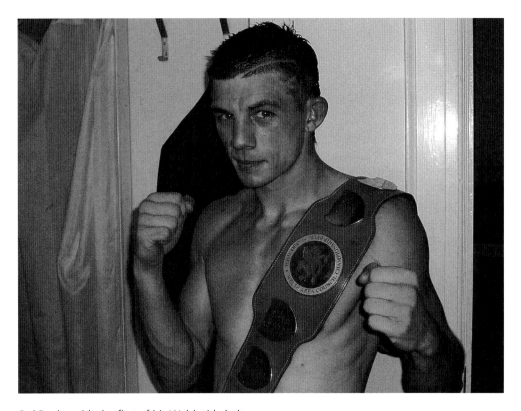

Dai Davies with the first of his Welsh title belts

Jason Booth, boxing binman Rendall Munroe, who won a European title two fights later, and, finally, Commonwealth Games gold medallist Jamie Arthur, who blasted an apprehensive Davies to defeat inside two rounds and took his Welsh belt. Dai's loss of direction was made worse by the tragic death of trainer Johnny Gamble.

After almost a year out, Davies returned at super-feather and claimed his second Welsh honour, halting well supported Cefn Fforest youngster Robbie Turley in nine rounds at the Newport Centre on June 6, 2009. The stoppage was prompted by a cut, but Davies had clearly shown his superiority.

But there followed another four defeats, three of them by stoppage, culminating, on October 30, 2010, in the loss of his national belt inside two rounds against Barry prospect Lee Selby, not normally regarded as a big puncher. Dai took time off to consider his future, though it seems he intends to box on.

DAI DOWER
(1933–)

🥊 **European Flyweight Champion   1955**

🥊 **Empire Flyweight Champion   1954–57**

🥊 **British Flyweight Champion   1955–57**

Dai Dower threw his first punches for cash at the age of four. Each Saturday night his father would kneel on the carpet of their terraced home in Herbert Street, Abercynon, and challenge his son to hit him on the nose – with a penny as the prize.

Dai remembers it well: "On Sunday mornings I'd get up with a shilling and he'd get up with a sore nose."

Later those same Sunday mornings, Dai senior and his fellow miners would gather in the Dower garden to cut each other's hair. Afterwards, they'd spar in a makeshift ring. The boy was hooked.

When he graduated to the real thing as an 11-year-old at the Roath Youth Club in Cardiff, it meant submission to the iron discipline of trainer Billy Mannings. And there was no chance of the curly-headed youngster ignoring the eight o'clock curfew just because he was out of sight back in Abercynon – the villagers made sure he kept to the schedule, with the local bobby dragging him out of the cinema at a quarter to eight just in case.

Not that Dai needed much encouragement. The pint-sized junior was so keen to fight that he wore specially made lead-lined slippers at weigh-ins to beat the rule that there should not be more than five pounds between opponents. But as he moved up the

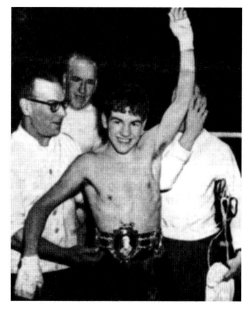

Dai Dower

Dai (right) takes on Anatoly Bulakov at the Helsinki Olympics

age groups, his weight barely altered, and more and more lead was needed. At 15 he was despatched to Uncle Charlie, a chef at a Bournemouth hotel, to be fattened up.

Success followed upon success, culminating in the 1952 ABA championship, and the Helsinki Olympics, where a Russian beat him on a dubious majority decision. It was the fourth and final defeat in Dower's 104 bouts as an amateur.

He turned pro in 1953 with Nat Seller, a former PTI in the RAF, known as a trainer of champions such as Harry Mizler, Eric Boon and Freddie Mills. Early on, it was plain sailing. A string of trial horses were left standing by the speed and mobility which had Seller lamenting the frequency with which his new charge wore out his boxing boots. Then, amid a forest of raised eyebrows, he took his place opposite Terry Allen himself. The man from Islington had briefly held the world title and was still champion of Britain. Three months short of his 30th birthday, Allen had 72 professional fights behind him, five at world championship level. Dai, still 20, had just 13.

In fact, it proved inspired matchmaking. In the second round, a crisp right buckled Allen's knees and another sent him to the canvas; the champion crawled pathetically about the ring, peering myopically towards his corner, and only responded to the referee's count when it was too late.

But it took another 18 months, and six more wins, before Dai was adjudged ready for his first title. The Empire flyweight champion had been taught boxing by a Catholic Brother from Yorkshire who discovered him as a 12-year-old in a black township of Johannesburg. Fanyana (Smallboy) N'Tuli had grown – though not much – to earn a worldwide reputation before removing the crown from the balding head of Hartlepool's Teddy Gardner two years earlier. But Jake Tuli, as he was now known, had just returned from Manila and a bad beating from Filipino Leo Espinosa. Now was the time to take him.

Dai and his proud mother

The preparation, however, had to be meticulous. Nat had Dai running five miles over the hills near his home for 12 days before he even laced on a glove. Then he cut out the roadwork altogether. It was a matter of getting him fit to start training, rather than trying to do the two simultaneously. For sparring in came Pat McCoy, formerly Tuli's gym companion. By the night of October 19, 1954, all was perfect.

The Harringay crowd were treated to an epic. Dower's straight left dominated the contest, the champion pinned on the end like a butterfly on display. Tuli pressed forward gamely, but the elusive challenger gave him no chance to deliver the left hook that had flattened a succession of foes. Dai was simply too fast and too clever.

The Welshman wept unashamedly as his hand was raised. In the dressing-room he was congratulated by Jimmy Wilde himself, downing a dozen bottles of orangeade while Mam fussed over his cut eye and the blisters like half-crowns he had acquired on the ball of each foot.

Dower faces South African rival Jake Tuli

Dai and manager Nat Seller

Flyweight idols past and present: Dai with the legendary Jimmy Wilde

The following day thousands packed the streets of Abercynon to welcome him home to the village where he was still earning £7 a week as a striker at the local colliery. He was chauffeured, as ever, by bus driver Eddie Davis, given time off for the task by his fight-loving bosses at Red and White.

Seller knew his young prodigy was ready for anyone, even world champion Yoshio Shirai. Jack Solomons fixed terms with the Japanese to risk his title at Harringay. But the Board of Control, heavily influenced by secretary Teddy Waltham, vetoed the match because Dai was not British champion. In fact, no-one was. Terry Allen had retired, and Dai had been paired with Eric Marsden to decide his successor.

"I think Waltham thought Eric would beat me, and wanted him to get any title chance going," recalls Dai. "In the end I met Marsden on February 8, 1955 – the day I should have been fighting Shirai."

By now, Dai's parents had taken over the Richards Arms at Cilfynydd, and he was able to train in the club room. It was not the only change in his circumstances. He announced that four days after the Marsden fight he was to marry teenager Evelyn Trapp, and he promised her the Lonsdale Belt as a wedding present.

In the event, it proved Dower's hardest contest to date. The Lancastrian, six inches taller and with a four-inch advantage in reach, was a different proposition from the tiny Tuli; he had a left jab of his own to keep Dai occupied in the early exchanges. The Welshman was forced to move inside, but adapted well and by the end of the fifth was beginning to take control. Marsden abandoned his own stylish boxing for two-fisted onslaughts, the steelworker from the Rugby League stronghold of St Helens sparing no effort to ensure that yet another Welsh dream went north. But Dower was again in command at the close, and Eric knew his exertions had been in vain. "Every time I thought I was going to get him," he said afterwards, "he just wasn't there."

After Dai had led the 4,000 Welshmen in the hall in *Hen Wlad fy Nhadau*, he and Evelyn revealed their secret. They had been wed a month earlier, and the new Mrs Dower showed how she had worn the wedding ring attached to her petticoat as she watched the fight from the Harringay balcony.

A month after the British title (with time out for a delayed honeymoon in Nice), Dai was to add the European. Nazzareno Giannelli, the champion from Padua, offered little resistance, backpedalling throughout the 15 rounds. His passivity silenced the 18,000 crowd at the Earls Court Exhibition Hall, and while Evelyn followed matters with avid interest, Signora Giannelli, in the next seat, kept her eyes closed throughout. She didn't miss much.

Now there was only one target left – Shirai, the first Japanese to win a world championship. But he had been held to a draw by a squat Argentinian called Pascual Pérez, and had promised him a title shot in Tokyo. Dower would have to mark time with a European defence against a mechanic from Madrid called Young Martín. They met at Nottingham Ice Rink and, for the Welshman, it was what the bullfighters call el momento de la verdad – the moment of truth.

His training had been less than thorough: personal and financial troubles had been a distraction, and he had injured a rib in sparring. That was the worst sort of handicap to take into the ring with a body-puncher like the Spanish southpaw. A left to the stomach put Dower on his knees in the fifth;

Evelyn watches her husband win the European crown, but the wife of champion Nazzareno Giannelli can't bear to look

Dower is out cold as Pascual Pérez celebrates his first-round victory

there were to be no fewer than 11 more visits to the canvas before the agony was ended in the 12th.

"Each time he caught me to the body it was like a knife," says Dai. "I'd go down, and after six or seven seconds the pain would pass, so I'd get up. Then he'd do it again. What annoyed me was the ref smiling when he was counting over me!"

Even in defeat, the little man's humour was intact. The following morning his father looked in and inquired how he felt. "The side's all right," Dai told him, "but my bloody knees are killing me!"

Dower could not believe what had happened, and paid repeated visits to the cinema to see the film of the fight that had so painfully scarred his pristine record.

Like the young cyclist who falls off his bike, he needed a quick return to action. There could have been easier opponents than old friend Jake Tuli, but Dai put his Empire laurels at stake against the former champion at Harringay just two months later. A right to the body sent the Welshman down in the fourth, but fortune favoured the brave and Dower came back strongly to take an easy victory. The hunt for a world title fight – now against Pérez, who had upset Shirai on his own territory – was back on.

It was successful, but at a price. Dai – by now Pte 23343412 Dower, D.W. – would have to tackle the champion in the bullring atmosphere of the San Lorenzo de Almagro Stadium in Buenos Aires.

Pérez, one of nine children, had built up his muscles in his father's hillside vineyard near Mendoza. He turned professional at 26, four years after winning Olympic gold in London in 1948. The draw with Shirai was the only blemish on his record, and while Fleet Street tried to convince its readers the Argentinian had never met anyone in Dower's class, in fact the reverse was true: Dai had never even seen a fighter as rough, determined and uncompromising as the tiny Pérez.

It would have been a hard task for a fit man, and Dower was far from that. Army food and ring idleness had sent his weight soaring: he was 10st 2lb when he learned the fight was to be in three weeks' time. It meant days lying in front of large fires in the barracks, wrapped in Army blankets. He barely ate

Teacher Dai shows his other sporting talents as a scrum-half to rugby players at his Bournemouth school

and his liquid intake was reduced to a minimum. Then, just as he was due to fly out, Dai heard that the contest had been postponed for a week; he rushed into a Cardiff café and drank 36 milk shakes. It put 10lb straight back on.

The sea journey to Argentina took three days, in increasing heat. "Everyone else in the party was pouring down the cold drinks and I had to watch them. I was so thirsty I could have drunk Jack Solomons's sweat!"

The three weeks before the bout were agony, despite the overwhelming friendliness of the local people. In the steak capital of the world, Dower was confined to boiled fish, and black, sugarless tea.

When he finally entered the ring on March 30, 1957, Dai was in no state to provide a serious challenge to a man who would be ranked among the all-time greats. A few light lefts at the start were all he offered to encourage the rich, Welsh-speaking sheep farmers who had flown in from the southern region of Patagonia. Pérez didn't even try to block them, concentrating on getting the Welshman into position for the left-right combination. Once he succeeded, it was a matter of time. The first one-two wobbled Dai, the second put him on the canvas, where he remained. Siesta for Dower, fiesta for Pérez. Two minutes and 48 seconds had been enough to end the first world title bid by a Briton in South America.

"I saw the right hand coming," remembers Dai. "It didn't look a knock-out punch and I just took it. The next thing I knew I was looking up at the lights."

It was effectively the end of a glittering career. Dower boxed just twice more, as a bantam, before turning to rugby, playing scrum-half for Bournemouth – still turning out in his forties – and becoming a P.E. teacher, first at a private school and then at Dorset Institute of Higher Education. The curly-headed kid who boxed with a grin is now a dapper man scaling hardly more than a stone above his fighting weight. And while his gallant, if hopeless challenge to Pérez will always be remembered, so too should the brilliance of the valley boy who captured three titles in less than five months.

JOHNNY EDMUNDS
(1902–1961)

🥊 Welsh Bantamweight Champion   1926–27

I f only he had taken the sport more seriously, the Treharris miner would have held his own with the best. That was the verdict of the trade paper, *Boxing News*, in 1926. And, although his name is inscribed proudly on the list of Welsh titleholders, there is still room for conjecture at what might have been had he attended the gym as often as he visited the pub.

In the early days, certainly, he was focussed enough. Barely a year into his pro career, the fresh-complexioned young man was already boxing for the vacant Welsh flyweight crown against Frank, the oldest of the fighting Kestrell brothers. At least, that's what the bills said.

Johnny Edmunds

Traditionalists dismissed the claim as absurd, because the bout in Barry was scheduled for a mere 15 rounds, rather than the usual championship distance of 20. Other sceptics pointed out the existence of many better qualified aspirants in those days before boxing had a generally recognised body to rule on such things. In the end it was pretty academic: the bout ended in a draw.

It was a thriller, however, unlike a rematch a month later in which Kestrell was said to have held repeatedly, but nevertheless emerged with the verdict. That time it was a 20-rounder, but not, seemingly, for the title. In any event, it was Edmunds's last outing at fly after needing a session in a Turkish bath in order to make the weight.

Fly or bantam, there was no shortage of useful opposition around and Johnny saw off the likes of Cardiff-based Ulsterman Minty Rose and Penygraig southpaw Gordon Cook, a future Welsh lightweight ruler, to earn himself a place in an official eliminator for the Welsh 8st 6lb belt. Working well inside, he outscored Rhondda boy Johnny Haydn and was rewarded with a shot at the reigning monarch, Sammy Jones, on Whit Monday 1925 at Pontypridd's Taff Vale Park.

It ended disastrously. Well on top, Edmunds floored the Ystrad man twice, but then threw another blow while the champion was still on one knee. Referee C.B. Thomas promptly disqualified him.

There were demands for a rematch, but it was not made until December 20, 1926, at Cardiff Hippodrome – and then Jones, citing medical advice, pulled out, vacating the throne. Young Evan Williams, from Tylorstown, was drafted in to replace him, but was outclassed. Edmunds was so much on top that he even helped Williams to his feet when he slipped over.

By now, Johnny was struggling to make bantam, particularly after several months' extended celebration of the birth of his first son, but he managed to shed the surplus for a defence against local teenager Tosh Powell on July 8, 1927, at Snow's Pavilion in Merthyr. The battle with the scales had clearly had its effect and Edmunds was down repeatedly, hampered further by a back strain picked up as he stumbled through the ropes in trying to avoid his tormentor. After 10 rounds, he retired on his stool.

He boxed sporadically for a few more years, a thickening waistline testimony to his dislike of training, but still held his own in decent company.

GEORGE EVANS
(1943–)

🥊 Welsh Lightweight Challenger   1968

With a father like Billy Evans, it was fairly inevitable that the youngster from Clare Street would end up in the ring. After all, Billy, a former pro himself, had become one of the best trainers in Merthyr, a place so steeped in boxing that even wrinkled grannies knew the difference between a left hook and a left cross.

George was only eight when Dad first took him to the upstairs gym at the old Angel Hotel building, later installing him as the first pupil of the Merthyr club he established, first at the Drill Hall, Georgetown, and then at various premises around the borough. Howard Winstone and Johnny Owen were among those who learned the basics from Billy.

A British Army Cadets title was the first evidence of his son's talent and those skills were carried on to senior level, where George won the Welsh ABA lightweight crown in 1965. He was still pondering offers to turn pro when the Welsh amateur selectors made up his mind for him, overlooking him for an important international.

The next dilemma was who to sign with. Evans opted for Mac Williams, a Cardiff docker just making his way in the fight game, while Billy continued to look after the training side. It began well, a hometown decision in Manchester the only loss in his first half-dozen outings. They also included an appearance before the National Sporting Club's dinner-jacketed audience at the Café Royal, where one ringsider was film star and ex-fighter Jack Palance, who was so impressed that he asked to meet the young Welshman afterwards.

The toffs who ran the place were pleased, as well. Evans became a regular performer in front of the cigar-smoking, champagne-quaffing members, who, by tradition, were silent during the rounds and released the tension in the intervals with little more than polite applause.

George Evans

George's father, former pro Billy Evans, at the Troedyrhiw gym

Only twice did George box in front of the rather less refined Welsh crowds, each time at the Afan Lido. The first visit saw him stop Bristolian Johnny Ratcliffe on the undercard of Winstone's all-Welsh British title showdown with Lennie 'The Lion' Williams. The second time he was bidding for a belt of his own, facing Llanharan's Bryn Lewis for the vacant Welsh lightweight honour.

Their meeting, on May 22, 1968, was a no-holds-barred battle which swung back and forth until coming to a premature end in the fifth, when Evans sustained a gash over the eye which prompted referee D.S. Davies to call a halt. There was to be no rematch and George played out the rest of his career in London rings, mostly on the dinner-boxing circuit.

The constant travelling began to pall, especially when fitted around a day job in the wages office at Dowlais steelworks, and Evans turned to training and management, opening a gym in a former infants school in Troedyrhiw and looking after the likes of Johnny Wall, who was to win the Welsh championship that eluded his mentor.

With the closure of the steelworks, George took over the Richards Arms in Abercanaid, while linking up with Aberdare-born former pro Paul Boyce to promote regular shows, mostly in the Neath and Swansea area. He then moved to Pembrokeshire, but, following the sad loss of wife Hilary, has now returned to live on his home patch.

BILLY EYNON
(1893–1980)

🥊 British Bantamweight Challenger   1920

The teenager from Treharris did not take long to learn the harsh truth about boxing economics. When Jack Scarrott set up his booth near Eynon's adopted home in Georgetown, he was tempted by the prospect of earning five shillings, proceeding to knock out one Tommy Stocking in the first round.

However, when he went to collect the cash the wily Scarrott told him that his cornermen, both, of course, in Jack's employ, were entitled to two bob each, leaving him just a shilling for his troubles. But Billy had made an impression on the booth-owner, who offered him a week's work at Brecon Fair. That extended to six months – and provided the collier boy with his basic education in the sport.

It was not plain sailing and one hammering at Tonypandy prompted Eynon to walk away. Fortunately, there were others with faith in the youngster's ability and he was persuaded to try again, being quietly fed a diet of pushovers to keep his confidence up.

World War I broke out before he had really established himself, but he kept active and even while serving with the Royal Artillery in France and Salonika there was time to lace up the gloves. He won the Army featherweight title in 1918 and met the Navy champion in Salonika before a crowd estimated at an incredible 200,000 people.

Back in civvy street – and down at his natural flyweight – Billy halted the useful Kid Doyle at Merthyr's Olympia Rink, despite having problems with his hair getting into his eyes. His seconds hacked off the offending strands before the sixth round and

Billy Eynon

The shell-shaped trophy Billy won before 200,000 people in Salonika

Eynon duly went out and finished the job with a body shot. The victory earned him a rematch at the National Sporting Club in an official eliminator for British honours. This time, however, the Salford man emerged with a points verdict. It was only when Billy stepped up to bantam that he was given another chance.

This time the dinner-jacketed patrons at the NSC watched as Eynon, dominant at close quarters, outboxed the taller, longer-limbed George Clarke. One judge somehow saw the Londoner ahead at the end, but the casting vote of referee 'Peggy' Bettinson saw Eynon go through to challenge British bantam king Jim Higgins in the same hall six weeks later, on November 29, 1920.

The 23-year-old Scot, from Hamilton, had won the vacant title with a controversial stoppage of Rhondda boy Harold Jones nine months earlier and the Eynon camp were confident. Manager Danny Davies promised that, as champion, his charge would take on all-comers, even Jimmy Wilde; he never had the opportunity. Billy, hampered by weight-making difficulties, was unable to capitalise on his height and reach advantages, Higgins rocking him in the ninth on the way to a points decision.

Not that everyone agreed with it. When the Prince of Wales and other wealthy ringsiders tossed gold sovereigns and white fivers into the ring at the end, an angry Danny Davies ordered Cardiff flyweight namesake Billy, assisting in the corner, to leave them, insisting, "We don't want their money – we want justice!" Eynon himself was more pragmatic, gladly accepting the cash thrust into his hands as he returned to the dressing room. "I think in the end I got more money than Higgins," he said, later. "But, of course, he had the belt."

Twice the pair were matched again, but each time the Scot pulled out with injury and Billy's hopes of revenge evaporated. He was awarded another

Snow's Pavilion, Merthyr (kindly lent)

A Grand Boxing Tournament

will be held at the above Pavilion

On Monday, March 5th, 1923,

For the Benefit of Billy Eynon.

Exhibition Boxing by
FRANK MOODY,
Cruiser Weight Champion, &

BEN MARSHALL,
Welter Weight Champion.

Also, 10 & 15 round Contests

Referee—Mr. JIMMY WILDE.
M.C.—Mr. F. H. CONDIE.

Doors open at 7, commence 7-30

Tickets, 2/4 inclusive

Ticket for a benefit show after Billy was forced to quit through eye trouble

eliminator a year later, however, against former world fly ruler Joe Symonds. It was a ding-dong tussle, with the Plymouth man in trouble in the 14th and Eynon suffering in the 16th, to be revived in the interval by a bottle of champagne poured over his head. It was just as well that the bout took place at the NSC; it is unlikely any bubbly would have been within reach at Merthyr Labour Club!

The judges disagreed, but once again Billy was the beneficiary of the referee's casting vote. But he never had his second shot at the title.

A detached retina, picked up in sparring, kept him sidelined for nearly two years. Although he had another half-dozen contests, his doctor was unhappy with the risk to his eyesight and he eventually listened to medical advice and called it a day.

MARTYN GALLEOZZIE
(1954–)

🥊 **Welsh Lightweight Champion   1976–77, 1978–1980**

Joe Calzaghe and Enzo Maccarinelli are merely the latest in a long line of Welsh boxers with Italian blood. One of the stars of the Welsh lightweight wars of the seventies is the great-great-grandson of an immigrant from the Bardi area, who set up shop in Merthyr in the 1870s making figurines for the church.

Martyn Galleozzie turns pro with a bearded Don James, watched by father Danny

Danny Galeozzi – the correct spelling – was the first of the family to box and it was he who introduced the nine-year-old Martyn to the sport at Billy Evans's Plymouth Street centre, just down the hill from his Twynyrodyn home. When this had to close, Danny established the Courthouse gym in the Labour Club, where his son was just one of an outstanding group of pupils, including a young Johnny Owen.

Martyn soon harvested Welsh schools and youth titles, followed in 1972 by success at senior level, when the apprentice carpenter reached the British final of the ABAs only to lose to George Turpin, who struck Olympic bronze in Munich a few months later.

Galleozzie then turned pro with Don James in the managerial chair, but his paid career could hardly have had a more disastrous

Galleozzie lands a right on a bloodied Johnny Wall in their mother of all battles

start. On a dinner show in Caerphilly, Martyn was stopped inside a round by Wolverhampton journeyman Billy Belnavis.

The Merthyr man showed that he, too, could bang a bit, winning his next two quickly, but then went against his manager's advice and accepted an Albert Hall date against former amateur star Vernon Sollas; the future British feather champion knocked him out in seven. That brought an end to his relationship with James and a retirement loss to another unbeaten youngster, Mario Stango, did nothing to improve his prospects.

Wily Cardiffian Mac Williams took over the reins, however, and a couple of wins – including revenge over Belnavis – earned Galleozzie a clash with Colin Miles for the vacant Welsh nine-stone crown. The Tonyrefail man, who had given up the bantam title because of problems making the weight, became a two-division champion with a fifth-round victory.

Over the next year or so, Martyn also had his difficulties with the scales and it was up at lightweight that he achieved his Welsh championship dream. After outpointing former amateur clubmate Johnny Wall in a 10-rounder at Treorchy, Galleozzie claimed the vacant belt on December 13, 1976, with a wide decision over Llantwit Major boy Dil Collins at the NSC.

The disputed verdict in his first meeting with Wall meant an inevitable rematch for the title – and their second showdown, at Rhydycar Leisure Centre on February 15, 1977, was an epic. The pair's commitment was demonstrated by a post-bell exchange after the first and, if referee Jim Brimmell kept a lid on the extra-curricular stuff from then on, there were plenty of legitimate shenanigans to keep the crowd in a ferment.

Galleozzie was sharper in the early stages, but Johnny took over in the middle sessions and looked in front going into the last. Yet the excitement continued to the end, with Martyn rocking his man with his trademark left hook only for the final gong, and the raising of Wall's arm, to come too soon.

A year off was followed by a couple of money-making trips to Scandinavia, before Galleozzie was given a shot at the man who had dethroned Wall, Rhondda boy Kelvin Webber, at the Afan Lido on July 10, 1978. Opting to box rather than fight, Martyn took the first two rounds before falling victim to the Porth fighter's body shots and visiting the canvas briefly in the fourth.

Kelvin's supremacy was short-lived, however, and the challenger regained control to take a 98–94 vote from Mr Brimmell.

The restored champion had a score to settle with his first defence, facing New Tredegar's Jeff Pritchard, a former featherweight challenger who had outpointed him two years earlier. He claimed his revenge at the Club Double Diamond, but it was hard work and Galleozzie needed a strong finish to edge referee Adrian Morgan's decision by half a point.

His good form earned the Merthyr man a British title final eliminator at a Windsor nightclub against unbeaten Scottish southpaw Dave McCabe. The skilful McCabe surprisingly opted to punch it out with the harder-hitting Galleozzie, but it worked well enough, and Martyn, bleeding badly from both eyebrows, was clearly second at the end.

Three more fights, three more defeats – all against decent foes – and further trouble with cuts brought the story to an end. These days boxing has long given way to golf for a man whose career provided a special chapter in the Welsh-Italian saga.

BILLY GRANELLY
(1911–1989)

🥊 Welsh Lightweight Challenger   1931

T he mis-spelling of the Pontypridd man's surname was not an error by
a slapdash reporter, but a deliberate choice. Billy's miner father, John,
who moved to Wales, like so many others, from the Northern Italian town of
Bardi, wanted his 12 children to merge into the host society and persuaded
his son to disguise his background. Like others in the family, he later reverted
proudly to the original Granelli.

By then Billy – and brother Cyril, who also boxed pro – had made the
amended version famous, at least locally. The lad from the Tramroad area of
the town established himself as a solid performer,
winning most, losing some, until a victory over
Welsh lightweight champion Gordon Cook put
him in pole position when the Penygraig southpaw relinquished his crown.

Granelly met Alby Kestrell for the vacant title
at the Engineers' Drill Hall in Cardiff's Newport
Road on August 31, 1931. It was an even tussle
in the early stages, but Billy was rocked in the
sixth and, from then on, his city rival took control and dominated the later rounds to earn a
comfortable decision from referee C.B. Thomas.

Billy had a run of draws before finishing the
year with a points loss to transplanted South
African George 'Panther' Purchase, whose success reflected that of the Springbok rugby side,
who beat Wales at a waterlogged St Helens a few
hours earlier.

It was more than two years before Granelly
had another sniff of the Welsh championship. He
was matched in an eliminator with Boyo Rees,
from Abercwmboi, a former victim, at Trealaw on
November 11, 1933. Billy tried to keep matters

*Billy Granelly, with brother and
trainer Louis*

Billy weighs in for his title bout with Alby Kestrell; manager Gomer Charles is on the far left

at long range, but the muscular Rees generally had the upper hand, cutting the Ponty boy in the fifth and then flooring him, only for the count to be interrupted at six by the sound of the bell. During the interval, the towel came in from the Granelly corner and it was announced, perhaps diplomatically, that Billy had injured a wrist.

There were no question marks, however, over the ankle problem that kept him out of the ring for nearly two years. But, even though he lost a close decision to Tredegar's Jack Phillips in his first fight back, contemporary reports suggest he displayed all his old skill before fading, understandably, towards the end.

The war, which saw him serve in the RAF, brought an end to his career and he settled in Barry, working on the town's docks. But there was a brief reminder of the past when Billy was among several former boxers questioned following the murder of their former manager, Gomer Charles, who was shot dead on answering the door of his Cardiff home in 1966.

Charles, an engine driver's son from Pontypridd who became a successful bookmaker after winning the Irish lottery, was not above the odd fiddle – indeed, he served time for his part in a horse-ringing scandal – so there were plenty of suspects. Given the mysterious non-arrival of some of their purses, ex-boxers were among them. In the end, it turned out the two men involved were ordinary burglars – and Billy was able to go back to his pint at Barry Conservative Club.

CHARLIE HAZEL
(1913–1981)

🥊 Welsh Flyweight Champion 1934–35

The lad from the Trallwn area of Pontypridd was known in his prime as 'The Welsh Wizard'. He was far from alone in being given that label, but if those who nicknamed him were lacking in originality, they could not be faulted in their assessment of what they saw.

The young Hazel – he somehow lost the second 'l' from his surname – was described as "nimble-witted and fleet-footed", armed with a fast, flicking left hand and the sort of elusiveness that seemed to come as standard from the Valleys' conveyor belt of flyweights.

Something else he had in common with many of his contemporaries (including big brother Billy) was an early start to his ring career, the necessity to learn on the job meaning a few losses in his mid-teens. But as he honed his skills, so the results began to go his way. People who had beaten him, such as cross-town rival Hector Alderman and Liverpudlian Johnny McGurn, were now on the receiving end.

His progress earned him a shot at Welsh fly king Herbie Hill, originally from Blaengwynfi, but based in Wembley, where he worked as a kennel lad for a greyhound trainer. They met at Cardiff's Greyfriars Hall on February 12, 1934, when Charlie was just emerging from his teens and the champion was five years older. It was an all-action scrap from the off.

Hazel's defence was, as ever, immaculate, but his tendency to slap incurred the wrath of referee C.B. Thomas as well as hindering his work. Hill, whose cleaner punches were decisive, showed sportsmanship when Charlie slipped in the seventh, allowing him to recover his balance rather than take advantage of his openness. A five-punch volley by Hill dropped Hazel in

Charlie Hazel

the ninth and he was down again as the bell rang. Charlie made a big effort in the last, but Hill again floored him twice and there was no argument with decision.

The pair met again at Merthyr Stadium on August 18, 1934. It was in many ways a similar contest, Charlie falling behind early on and dropped in the fifth by a borderline body shot, but this time his pure skill overcame Herbie's heavier punching. The Afan Valley man fought desperately to keep his crown, but this time Hazel kept on the move and picked up points on the counter. There was little doubt about F.R. Hill's decision.

Charlie never defended the belt, content to travel around Britain and capitalise on the extra earning power that came with the title. There were some good scalps: Jimmy Warnock, pride of the Shankill, outpointed in Belfast, revenge over future British fly champion Bert Kirby. But there were an increasing number of quick defeats, not least a two-round blitz at the hands of the legendary Benny Lynch, who won the world title four months later.

After that he boxed mainly at home, where old foe Hill had reclaimed the belt, but there was no rubber match.

Charlie worked in haulage for a while before the war, later moving to Kent, where he married and raised a family before his death at the age of 67.

KERRY HOPE
(1981–)

🥊 Welsh Light-Middleweight Challenger   2009

Many boxers have dreamed of fighting in America. But dreams can so easily turn into nightmares.

The chance to tag along with stablemate and sparring partner Joe Calzaghe and box in the historic ring at Madison Square Garden must have seemed the fulfilment of a fantasy. Then it all went wrong.

Bill-toppers Calzaghe and Roy Jones, Jr, made the weight successfully before their November 2008 showdown. So did Kerry Hope. But his proposed foe was five and a half pounds over the agreed figure. It was too much for Hope's trainer, Enzo Calzaghe, who promptly pulled the Merthyr man out. Watching friend Joe put on a masterclass for the New York crowd was no consolation.

The following year, having left the Calzaghe set-up, Kerry headed west to California and linked up with locally based Englishman John Tandy in a bid to revive his career. A straightforward points win over Daniel Stanislavjevic helped, but Tandy then matched him with an unbeaten local in St Paul, Minnesota, for the spurious WBF International super-middle belt, two divisions above the Welshman's usual weight. Shaven-headed Caleb Truax, with 13 straight wins and a *Boxing Digest* Prospect of the Month, ran out a clear-cut points victor – at least, according to the Minnesotan judges. It was the end of another American adventure.

Hope, from Galon Uchaf, was born to boxing. The grandson of the legendary

Kerry Hope

The cut that ended Hope's Welsh title dream

(or notorious, depending on your point of view) Malcolm Price, he first laced on the gloves at 12 and developed his skills at Dowlais ABC, but was a nearly man as an amateur, losing to Swansea boy Dale Rees in his only senior final. The pro scene proved much more to his liking.

With Frank Warren promoting the Calzaghe stable, regular and lucrative work was guaranteed and the young southpaw responded with 11 victories on the trot. However, most came against travelling survivors and in no way prepared him for the sudden leap in class when he faced big-punching Mancunian Matthew Hall at Cardiff International Arena. Despite having only one stoppage to his name, he rashly opted to slug it out with a slugger. The outcome was predictable: Hope was floored in the third and seventh, before being rescued in the eighth.

Hall went on to halt another Calzaghe man, Bradley Pryce, capturing the Commonwealth crown, while Kerry stagnated, the near-miss in New York the closest he came to action in 11 months, as the bitter split between Warren and the Calzaghes hit the gym hard.

When Enzo entered the promotional field himself, Hope headed the card against Abercynon rival Taz Jones with the vacant Welsh light-middle title at stake. In his first paid appearance in his home town, on February 21, 2009, at the newly rebuilt Rhydycar Leisure Centre, his expected coronation was wrecked by an eyebrow gash that prompted referee Wynford Jones to end matters in the fourth of an evenly balanced contest, in which Taz had caused the favourite plenty of problems even before the injury.

The anticipated rematch never materialised and Hope hit the road for Los Angeles. Since returning home, he has been left in limbo. But he insists the story is not yet over.

LEN 'ROCKY' JAMES
(1933–2011)

🥊 Welsh Heavyweight Challenger   1965

Everybody in Pontypridd knew 'Rocky'. But not as a boxer. No, to the people of the town he was Jenny James's brother.

When Jenny hit the headlines in 1951 as the first Welsh swimmer to conquer the English Channel – she was also the first from anywhere to manage a double crossing of the Bristol Channel – kid brother Leonard had not even laced on a glove. And, while many boxers drift away from the sport after getting hitched, it was marriage which led to 'Rocky' taking it up.

Home cooking added a few pounds to the James physique and he headed to a gym in Bristol, where he was working as a foreman in a sack factory, to sweat off the surplus. There he met boxing coach Basil Withers and was persuaded to give it a try.

Within weeks he was doing it for real, beginning an amateur career that saw him reach three successive British ABA finals only to come second each time, twice hampered by damaged hands. His third defeat came at the hands of popular East Ender Billy Walker, later to pack them in as a professional, though James did beat the 'Blond Bomber' once on his own club show at West Ham.

Having finally won the 1962 Welsh ABAs – he was twice runner-up – he earned a trip to Perth for the Empire and Commonwealth Games, but was controversially disqualified

Len 'Rocky' James

for a low blow against Ugandan George Oywello in the quarter-final. With only five entrants at heavyweight, Oywello went on to strike gold; it could so easily have been the boy from Wood Road.

Instead Len turned pro with Cardiff manager Benny Jacobs. He was already over 30 and had no time to work his way up the ladder. After a debut victory when Midlander Charlie White was turfed out for persistent holding, it was straight in with the big boys. Londoner Len Hobbs, a top amateur and unbeaten as a pro, beat him twice in a row, and Midlander Ron Gray, later a manager and promoter, also came out on top.

Rocky in later years

Another to outpoint him was a successor as Welsh amateur heavy king, Carl Gizzi, a Rhyl boy who was based in Merthyr with Eddie Thomas, but James did well enough for the pair to be matched again for the vacant Welsh title. Their first clash had been at the functional Drill Hall in Cardiff's Dumfries Place; the second took place beneath the chandeliers of the Café Royal in rather more fashionable Piccadilly on June 28, 1965.

Gizzi, 11 years younger and with 14 straight wins behind him, lived up to his status as hot favourite. His speed helped him avoid Len's increasingly desperate swings and referee Harry Gibbs did not help with frequent lectures to the frustrated Treforest man. A right to the heart dropped 'Rocky' early in the fifth and when Carl stormed in to finish it, Mr Gibbs took the hint and called a halt.

James carried on, always giving value for the punter's pound, for another three years, announcing his retirement on his 36th birthday. He and his four children moved to Cornwall following his wife's untimely death through cancer and he earned a crust diving for sea urchins, which he polished and sold to gift shops. But hiraeth brought him back to Treforest, where he lives in Alexandra Road, not far from where the story started. And, at 77, he is still fit enough to play four rounds of golf a week. But hiraeth brought him back to Treforest, where he lived in Alexandra Road until his death on the eve of his 78th birthday.

ROY JOHN
(1947–2007)

🥊 British and Commonwealth Light-Heavyweight Challenger 1973

Nelson is a name renowned in boxing history. Azumah of that ilk was one of the all-time great featherweights. Johnny may not have hit quite those heights, but a six-year reign as WBO cruiser king is pretty good for someone who lost his first three pro fights. And from a Welsh perspective, there was Roy John, who carried the label of his sleepy home village around the world.

In fact, the globe-trotting light-heavyweight originally came from Abercynon, only moving to Nelson after marrying Anne in 1969. Academically educated at Carnetown, his fistic lessons came in the gyms of Pontypridd and Dowlais, as he pursued an amateur career which yielded a British junior championship and three Welsh ABA victories, also seeing him represent his country at the Europeans in Rome.

When the time came to swap medals for money, there was only one door to knock on. Eddie Thomas duly signed Roy up and he made his debut, a points win over Bristol-based Jamaican Dervan Airey, in the opening bout before the second Howard Winstone-Vicente Saldívar showdown at Ninian Park.

Roy John

Despite a cuts loss next time out, there was steady progress as the young plasterer – campaigning at middleweight, despite his amateur successes coming up at light-heavy – mixed contests across South Wales with regular visits to the National Sporting Club's HQ at London's Café Royal. It was soon time to talk of titles.

And even though John dropped a close decision to Cardiffian Dick Duffy at the NSC, it was the valley boy who was matched with another city slicker, Carl Thomas, for the vacant Welsh throne. Thomas had home advantage, at Sophia Gardens Pavilion, and referee Joe Morgan also hailed from the capital. With the official on

Roy (left) works in close with Tim Wood in their British title final eliminator

Roy's case for holding, there was more than a little controversy when he raised Carl's arm at the end.

John did not box for another seven months, returning at light-heavy, and seemed to be set for life as a run-of-the-mill operator, especially as he was repeatedly hampered by loose bone chippings in his left elbow. There were no fewer than four fights in just over a year against Jamaican Lloyd Walford, three of them lost, and the first of Roy's lucrative ventures to mainland Europe and South Africa.

There were now new men in the corner, with Howard Winstone in charge of training at Penydarren and Scot Bobby Neill holding the managerial reins. The change paid dividends when John was matched with Johnny Frankham in an official final eliminator for the British title. The Reading gipsy was a hot favourite at the first bell at the York Hall, but Roy kept plugging away and his workrate earned him the verdict. It was the Welshman who would take on Chris Finnegan at Wembley Pool on March 13, 1973, with the St Ives man's Commonwealth crown also on the line.

The Olympic gold medallist was at a crossroads, coming off two losses, both in the same hall. The outstanding Bob Foster had knocked him out in 14 rounds of a battle for the WBC and WBA light-heavy straps, before

Finnegan lost his European honour when a badly split nose meant a 12th-round stoppage loss to German Rudiger Schmidtke. Even though Chris had been ahead on all three cards on that occasion, he was said to be sluggish and well below par, and there were suggestions that a loss to John would see him hang up his gloves.

Finnegan, encouraged from ringside by voluble wife Cheryl, undaunted by being eight and a half months pregnant, dispelled all doubts with a confident performance, even if a slow start saw the pre-fight odds of 5–2 on the champion drift to evens by the end of the fourth. The southpaw with the mutton-chop sideburns moved further and further clear from the halfway stage to win comfortably, even if the margin – referee Wally Thom gave the challenger only one round – was ludicrously unfair.

"I thought I won the first few rounds easily, a bit too easily," lamented Roy. "He won it all right, but I can't say I agreed with the scoring."

The authorities certainly approved of his showing and included the Welshman – now managed by Reading-based Bev Walker – in another final eliminator, this time against Leicester's Tim Wood in front of a full house at the Club Double Diamond. Wood, five years younger at 23, was cut along the left eyebrow from the fifth, but repeatedly hurt Roy with big right hands, only for John to storm back. This time referee Thom saw things his way.

He was never to get a return with Finnegan, however. Both men had eye problems, in the champion's case a detached retina which forced him into retirement. John, whose trouble involved the muscle controlling the eye movement, was finally allowed to box on after 18 months' inactivity.

Walker was in talks regarding a shot against the new titleholder, Bunny Johnson, but as no contracts had yet materialised, he felt able to accept a big-money purse to face Ugandan Mustapha Wassaja in Denmark. The Board warned that if Roy lost they would have to reconsider his suitability as a challenger, but nobody expected him to get stopped in five rounds. The disappointed Welshman promptly called it a day.

JOE JOHNS
(1892–1927)

Welsh Lightweight Champion   1915

Joe Johns

There were those who, marvelling at the Merthyr boy's power and athleticism, tipped him to go all the way to a world title. But his physical perfection masked an adversary as determined as any he met in the ring. Rheumatism, aggravated by his time in the trenches, was to prove too strong.

If his international ambitions were curtailed by ill-health and World War I, there was no shortage of success on the domestic scene, with Johns – the final 's' stuck around throughout his career, even though his actual surname was John – claiming Welsh titles at various weights.

Back in the days before the National Sporting Club standardised the classes, there were championships up for grabs at two-pound intervals and, just to make things even more confusing, fight reports rarely agreed on which particular honour was at stake. At one time or another, Joe claimed Welsh supremacy in four different divisions.

He was barely 15 when he won a competition at just six stone, but had filled out to 8st 8lb when he won his first national recognition in February 1910 with a disqualification win over Pontypool's Young Walters, a victory he repeated on points the following month.

By the end of a busy year, Johns had avenged a knockout defeat by Cardiff-based American seaman Battling Harris and outscored Matthewstown southpaw Fred Edwards to stake a claim to the Welsh title at 9st 4lb, a crown he defended against Ebbw Vale's Jack Sugrue. But by the end of 1911 the rheumatism was beginning to leave its mark.

Defying medical orders to rest, Joe lost a showdown with Midlander Tommy Mitchell in Sheffield for the British pitmen's championship and was similarly outpointed by local

Joe's grave, with correct spelling

Nat Williams in Liverpool. Even when he took a break from actual contests, Johns still indulged in exhibitions with mentor Jim Driscoll whenever charity called. Things could have been worse: he and the Peerless One were due to travel to the US, only for the trip to be cancelled. They had been booked to sail on the *Titanic*.

Back to fitness, Joe took aim at the now properly constituted Welsh light-weight title at its new 9st 9lb limit, outpointing Tirphil's Arthur Evans in a 20-round final eliminator before 4,000 at Merthyr Drill Hall and earning a crack at champion Dai Roberts, from Caerau, at Tonypandy Pavilion in February 1914. The bout ended in chaos.

After 17 evenly fought rounds, the referee, Mr J.W. Thwaites, from the NSC, who had been standing outside the ring smoking a cigarette, climbed through the ropes and halted the action. He claimed that the constant inter-ruptions by one of Johns's seconds, trying to draw his attention to infringe-ments by Roberts, had proved such a distraction that he was not prepared to risk his reputation by giving a verdict. So he pronounced it 'No Contest'.

When Roberts gave up the belt to step up to welter, Johns was matched with Evans to decide his successor, but had to pull out with a return of his muscular pain. When he recovered, he shed the rust with a repeat success over Fred Edwards, but three days later Britain declared war on Germany.

Although married with a family – and despite his medical history – Joe signed up with the Royal Engineers, but on May 22, 1915, finally had his date with Evans in front of 10,000 fans at Cardiff Arms Park. With a silver challenge cup and a suit also up for grabs, the Merthyr man took referee Eugene Corri's points decision.

He was to wear the crown for just two months (the suit lasted rather longer). Both Joe and Evans were now in khaki and stationed on Merseyside, so it was at the famous Liverpool Stadium that the pair met on July 22. The referee, Wales's reigning British welter champion Johnny Basham, another serving soldier, warned Arthur for hitting on the break in the fourth and counted seven over him in the eighth as Johns controlled matters. But Evans bounced back in a sensational scrap and when he decked Joe right on the bell to end the 16th, the champion was unable to emerge for the next.

Four years in France did little for Johns's health and although he had one attempt to prolong his career after hostilities ended, he was beaten in 13 rounds by Aberdare's Danny Arthurs. That was it. Just eight years later he died of pneumonia in Merthyr Infirmary and was buried at Cefn Coed "with little Joe his son".

GERALD JONES
(1943–)

🥊 Welsh Bantamweight Champion   1966–68

There were few surprises in the career of the miner from Pengarnddu. In 36 professional contests, he met only 16 different opponents. He even faced Wigan-based North Walian namesake Gerry Jones four times, which must have been pretty confusing for ringsiders.

But he is best remembered for his trilogy of Welsh title fights with Cardiffian Terry Gale, over a 13-month period in the mid-1960s.

The historic rivalry between city slicker and valley boy was probably lost on the dinner-jacketed patrons of the National Sporting Club, where the pair met for their first argument on June 28, 1965. But they knew a good scrap when they saw one – and this collision for the vacant Welsh bantam throne certainly qualified.

Jones overcame a sluggish start to take control in the middle rounds, only for Gale to stage a late recovery and snatch the belt with a close, but undisputed points verdict.

On September 23 they were at it again. This time it was on home soil, at least for the champion, at Sophia Gardens Pavilion. But even a Cardiff crowd and a Cardiff referee, Joe Morgan, did not help Terry to victory, even if he did keep hold of his crown. A similarly see-sawing collision ended in a draw, with the enthralled punters throwing cash on to the canvas in appreciation of what they had seen.

It was inevitable that they would meet for a third time, although it was not until July 12, 1966 that the pair came face to face again at the Afan Lido. This time there was a major

Gerald Jones

departure from the usual script. After starting strongly, Gale suffered a broken jaw in the sixth. Although he said nothing and carried gamely on, once manager Mac Williams realised, two rounds later, he pulled his man out. Jones was the champion.

But the Merthyr boy's celebrations were mixed with compassion for his victim. The fight had been made on a winner-take-all basis, but Gerald, perhaps sensing that Terry's injury would effectively end his career, insisted that the two should share the money.

The win was the pinnacle of a career which began as a nine-year-old, taken to Eddie Thomas's boxing academy to add some lustre to fighting skills already evident on the now demolished streets of Pengarnddu. The maestro's touch guided Jones to Welsh honours at schools, youth and senior levels, before he turned pro following a dispute with the Welsh ABA over international selection.

With Thomas's hand still on the tiller, Gerald – who also worked at his mentor's private mine – was kept busy and, if losses were as frequent as victories, he picked up some notable scalps, particularly that of British title challenger Tony Barlow, still regarded by Jones as his toughest opponent.

"I boxed him the evening before I was married," he recalls. "The following day I could barely speak – and as for the wedding night..."

Ironically, the title triumph was the last time Jones's arm would be raised. He was halted in five rounds by big-punching Ghanaian Sammy Abbey and took 20 months off before returning under the guidance of Empire Games medallist Roger Pleace. There were four more bouts, all lost on points, before Gerald retired and turned to training. And he is still at it, producing a string of amateur champions.

TAZ JONES
(1982–)

🥊 Welsh Light-Middleweight Champion   2009–2010

Some boxers are remembered less for the fights they win than for those they lose. Or, in the case of the scaffolder's son from Ynysboeth, a contest he won in the eyes of everyone who saw it – except for the referee.

Jones faced Pontypool's Tony Doherty, once a team-mate in Wales's Commonwealth Games team, at Cardiff International Arena on September 10, 2005, with the vacant Celtic welterweight belt at stake. 'The Doc', with a 15-bout unbeaten streak as a pro, was generally tipped to claim the first title in a glittering career. Well, he did. But even he knew it was a travesty.

The lanky Jones, bursting with confidence, strode the ring in complete control for the first four rounds as an off-colour Doherty struggled to get inside his long left hand. Tony was soon bleeding from the nose and it was the second half of the 10-rounder before he began to have any success. A good sixth was followed by a tentative seventh and only when Taz started to tire did Doherty take command.

A few rights began to get through and the favourite dominated the closing session, but Jones seemed to have built up a more than adequate lead early on. Not in the eyes of referee Lee Cook, who voted 98–94 for 'The Doc', giving only two rounds to Taz. It was an unbelievable scoreline and deserved the derision with which it was greeted.

But that was little consolation to the Cynon Valley man. And when the pair met again at the Millennium Stadium on April 7, 2007, things were very different. This time Doherty came out like a train, rocked Jones in the opener and wore him down until referee Roddy Evans made a compassionate stoppage after Taz was floored in the seventh.

Taz Jones

It all began for Lee Jones – he was dubbed 'Taz' as a child for a perceived resemblance to a Tasmanian Devil – at Gilfach Goch ABC, though he soon switched to the local Kyber Colts club, whose coach, Brian Coleman, continued to guide him as a pro. A sideboard full of trophies as a junior was followed by a senior Welsh title in 2002, the year he went to the Manchester Commonwealth Games only to be drawn in his first bout against England's Paul Smith, who went on to win silver and later become Britain's pro super-middle champion.

Opting to punch for pay himself, Jones made a stuttering start with two draws, but had suffered only one loss – to Matthew Hatton, Ricky's kid brother and now himself a world-class operator – before taking the British Masters light-middle crown from holder Kevin Phelan in only his 11th outing. He then travelled to Edinburgh to face unbeaten local Colin McNeil for the Celtic honour, only to lose on points.

Dropping down to welter, he suffered that disappointment against Doherty and, after their second encounter, moved back to the 11st class. After shocking Plymouth's Carl Drake with a one-round demolition job to acquire the so-called International Masters belt, Jones was halted by hard-hitting Matthew Hall and unbeaten Pole Grzegorz Proksa before facing Merthyr boy Kerry Hope for the vacant Welsh title on the inaugural Calzaghe Promotions card at Rhydycar Leisure Centre on February 21, 2009.

Taz belied his recent form to cause Hope all sorts of problems, but supremacy was still up for grabs when a clash of heads in the second session left both men cut. Kerry's injury was by far the worse, however, and by the fourth had deteriorated sufficiently for referee Wynford Jones to call it off.

The obvious rematch fell apart over money and Taz was to have only one more contest, a points loss to another Jones boy, the self-styled Prince Arron, before queries over his medicals brought him a suspension from the Board. He chose not to appeal and, instead, turned to the cage-fighting scene.

NATHAN KING
(1981–)

🥊 World Super-Middleweight Challenger   2004

Talk about jumping in at the deep end! When the 19-year-old scaffolder from Mountain Ash made his paid debut, it was not in front of his home crowd against some unambitious journeyman. Instead he climbed through the ropes at the spiritual home of British boxing, the York Hall in London's East End, to face Tony Oakey, a two-time English ABA champion with nine straight wins behind him as a pro.

Not that King was at all fazed. He stood up to the more experienced Portsmouth fighter and earned the plaudits of the game's most knowledgeable spectators as he restricted Oakey to a two-point margin.

His performance came as no surprise to those who keep tabs on the youngsters on the Welsh scene. After taking up the sport at 12 with Brian Coleman's Kyber Colts club, Nathan collected a string of Welsh schoolboy titles – and a Gaelic Games gold medal – before adding Welsh ABA senior honours at middle and light-heavy.

He began punching for pay after a row with amateur officialdom – a familiar story in Wales – signing with Frank Warren and Enzo Calzaghe, who knew him well from sparring sessions with his son, Joe. It was a role he continued to occupy for much of his early career, something a few critics have suggested hampered his own development, although recurrent elbow problems also played their part.

After his harsh baptism against Oakey, Nathan won six in a row, three on return visits to his appreciative new fans in Bethnal Green. He was also parading his wares at home, on the undercards of his regular sparmate. It was on one such bill, at Cardiff Castle, that King, forced to wait until around midnight, dropped another decision, to French West Indian Valéry Odin.

His career entered something of a sticky patch with five losses in half a dozen bouts, one to future Commonwealth boss Ovill McKenzie. But a recovery in his form earned a world title shot, of sorts. The Cynon Valley man was matched with London-based Georgian Eric Teymour at the Hilton Hotel on Mayfair, on November 24, 2004, with a vacant WBU belt at stake.

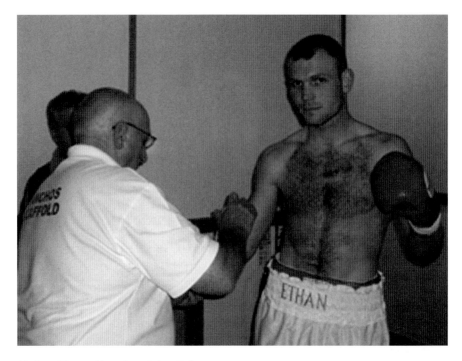

Nathan King, with trainer Brian Coleman

As if facing the big-hitting southpaw from Tbilisi – he had lost only once in 18 contests, stopping nine of his victims – was not enough, the showdown was at super-middle, calling for Nathan to come in almost a stone lighter than in his previous outing. It did not help the Welshman as he tackled the bull-like Teymour, but he battled on to survive the 12 rounds, only to find the three judges scoring against him by margins of six, eight and nine points.

Since then King has twice tried for Celtic honours at 12st, losing to unbeaten Scots Stevie McGuire – a former amateur victim – and Kenny Anderson.

But he has mainly been used as a trial horse, a man who can be relied upon to test those being groomed for greater things. He was outscored in a rematch with Oakey, who had been both WBU and Commonwealth champion since they first met. Former and future British super-middle rulers Tony Dodson and Tony Quigley also came out on top, while unbeaten Frenchman Jean-Paul Mendy forced Nathan to retire in six in Paris.

Mendy had boxed at the Atlanta Olympics and recently King has found himself facing two of Britain's successful squad from Beijing. Gold medallist James DeGale and bronze winner Tony Jeffries each had to settle for points, but another stand-out amateur, Cuban world junior champion Luis Garcia, ended things in five rounds.

FRANK MOODY
(1900–1963)

- British Middleweight Champion   1927–28

- British Light-Heavyweight Champion   1927–29

T he first Welshman to win British titles at two weights, the eldest son of a fighting family might have added world laurels had it not been for his fragile hands. As it was, he could be proud of his achievements in a 22-year career on both sides of the Atlantic.

And his successes between the ropes were matched by an unassuming demeanour when off-duty, earning him American praise as "possibly the finest boxing ambassador Britain ever sent to the US".

Born and raised at Trallwn, near the old bridge in Pontypridd, Frank was the oldest of 13 children born to miner and mountain fighter George. Four of his seven brothers boxed professionally – two winning Welsh titles – but he always claimed that as a boy his best sparring partner was sister Lizzie.

An incident at school, which ended with young Frank knocking a classmate into the canal, prompted Dad to begin teaching him the rudiments of the game and, already fascinated by the regular visits of Jack Scarrott's booth, it was inevitable he would take up the sport himself. Appropriately, Scarrott's marquee – though pitched at Tonypandy – was the scene of his first proper bout, when he was 13, and it came against a world champion!

At least, Kid Evans, of Trehafod, claimed the 5st 6lb title, although it is doubtful if the "world" extended beyond the Taff and Rhondda valleys. Moody closed one of the Kid's eyes and had virtually shut the other by the final bell, when the newcomer's arm was raised in victory. The winner pocketed both purse and sidestake, so

Frank Moody

Frank was throwing punches at an early age

Frank and wife Lily

Frank persuaded his father to pay a doctor to lance the swellings for the penniless Evans to find his way home.

Frank had scaled 5st 12lb, so the Kid's "title" was not at stake. No matter. He would take on a real world champion before his time was up.

On reaching 14 he became eligible to work underground and became a trolley-boy, hauling the trams of coal, an exercise which helped put muscles on his skinny frame.

Although he lost as often as he won, he was learning on the job. And his basic talent already shone through. When he outpointed Young Riley, the West of England fly champion, in Plymouth, the bout was refereed by the editor of *Boxing*, John Murray, who told the young Welshman that he expected him to become a champion.

His progress was such that he needed a proper manager, linking up with Wyndham Williams, and began training at the famous gym attached to the Greenmeadow Hotel in his home town.

The coming of peace meant Moody no longer had to work in the pits, so he became a full-time boxer. His first belt soon followed. As he moved through his teens, he had piled on the pounds and now challenged Welsh middle champion Wyndham Price at the Mill Field Athletic Ground, Pontypridd, on May 3, 1919. It didn't last long. Frank rocked the Newbridge veteran at the end of the first and, although the bell saved him, he told his cornermen he wanted no more. Frank celebrated by marrying girlfriend Lily two days later.

They began a fortnight's honeymoon amid the bright lights of Cardiff, only for their break to be interrupted by an offer of a 20-round fight at the Blackfriars Ring. The money was good, so Lily headed back to Ponty and her new husband travelled to London – to be knocked out by Bermondsey Billy Wells.

His journeys across the border brought mixed success and the low point arrived against former world welter king Ted 'Kid' Lewis. The first gong was still echoing around Manchester's

Frank spars with brother Glen

Free Trade Hall when two lefts and a right hook dropped Frank on his face. The Welshman rolled over and tried to rise, but fell back to be counted out. It was all over in a mere 16 seconds.

"The money – £125 – was the best I'd ever been paid and like a chump I fell for it," recalled Frank later. "I had to lose half a stone. I was so weak I had to be held up to get on the scales."

When his father was hurt down the pit, Moody needed a new trainer and he turned to a man who would become a lifelong friend, Llew Williams, then mine host at the Ruperra Hotel, along Berw Road from Pontypridd's present-day bus station. Llew urged him to sign with influential manager Teddy Lewis and, with no contract tying him to Wyndham Williams, he made the switch.

Teddy soon put out a £100-a-side challenge to any British middleweight except his namesake, the 'Kid'. Shoeing-Smith Fred Davies accepted. They had met twice before, each winning once, so it was agreed to meet at Pontypridd's Taff Vale Park, with Moody's Welsh middle title at stake.

Frank and manager Billy Ames

Frank knew all about Davies by now and dominated throughout until the ref stepped in to rescue the Llanelli man in the 16th.

With no immediate prospects at middle, Frank beat a couple of light-heavies and began to eye that belt instead. But he had to punch harder to put a dent in the bigger boxers and his hands began to rebel against the extra workload. Both were damaged in a points loss to Belfast policeman Dave Magill in Liverpool, but, with a wife and two little girls to support, there was no way he could take time off for them to heal properly.

Despite his handicap, Moody beat future Empire heavyweight king Larry Gains in five rounds and outscored Australian George Cook despite conceding two stone. He also saw off fellow-Welshman Gipsy Daniels in Newport on a lucky night for Llew. The trainer took time off from Tymawr Colliery, Hopkinstown, to work the corner; while he was away, there was a roof fall at the pit and the man who had replaced him was among four who died.

Plans were now in train for Frank to try his luck in the States, and, after confirming his Welsh supremacy with another victory over Shoeing-Smith Davies, he sailed on the *Berengaria*, with Llew, stablemate Francis Rossi, Lancastrian Ted Marchant and Billy Ames, who had contacts in New York and would manage them there.

After a few impressive wins, the call came for Moody to meet Tommy Loughran at Madison Square Garden in what was effectively a world title eliminator; unfortunately, British champion Roland Todd arrived in New York and pointed out that he had kayoed the Welshman. The promoters promptly put the Doncaster boxer in with Loughran and Frank had to settle for a spot on the undercard.

There was to be no short cut to the top, but the Pontypridd man was able to carve out a decent living. There were also a few events which, in the words of the yet unborn Don King, could happen "only in America".

When Moody faced Joe Jackson in Wilkes-Barre, Pennsylvania, where he was supported by a large contingent of expatriate Welsh miners, the fight ended in chaos. Matchmaker Al Dewey, a former pro, became so fed up with referee J.B. Kelly's inability to get Jackson to break clean that in the seventh he climbed through the ropes, turfed the official out and proceeded to take over. When he separated them and pushed Jackson back, that worthy thumped him; Dewey punched back and police had to jump into the ring to end the fracas before telling the crowd to go home. No result was ever given.

Lou Bogash, known as 'The Blond Italian', claimed never to have been floored in 175 fights. Deluded by his presumed indestructability, he stuck his chin out and invited Frank to punch it. He did so – and kept doing so until the referee had to haul him off. The following day the local mayor came around to see Moody, but not to congratulate him: he wanted a new straw hat to replace the one ruined when Ames, in the Welshman's corner, drenched it each interval as he waved a sodden sponge at his charge. The civic dignitary was advised to buy an umbrella.

Ames was sometimes a little over-enthusiastic in finding fights and Frank found himself booked to face No 1 contender Jock Malone and world champion Harry Greb within four days.

Malone was so confident that he told local pressmen in Boston that if he lost he would jump into Massachusetts Bay. After a mediocre bout, Moody was declared the winner, but Jock left town without the promised leap. In fairness, when he returned to the city and lost again, he did indeed throw himself fully clothed off the Charleston Bridge. And, when he was fished out of the water, he climbed back on to the parapet and jumped again. "That's the one I owed Moody," he explained.

Meanwhile Frank had travelled to Connecticut to face Greb in their non-title encounter. Not for nothing was the champion regarded as one of the filthiest fighters who ever lived. Harry came straight out, grabbed Moody's neck with his left hand and repeatedly rubbed the laces of his right glove across his face, leaving him bleeding badly. Harry used his elbow, back-handers and in the third gouged Moody's right eye; Moody shouted in pain and stepped back, his hand over the injury, and Greb promptly floored him with a right hand.

Frank did OK in the next couple of sessions, but in the sixth Greb thumbed him again, the ref ignored his protests and he was floored once more. This time he attempted to rise at seven, but stumbled and his hand briefly renewed contact with the boards. Harry cried, "He's out!" The third man agreed and waved it over. A ringside photographer later said the timing device on his camera indicated the complete count lasted just six seconds.

"I knew I'd never get a shot at the title all the time Greb held it," confessed Frank. "And, quite frankly, I didn't mind a bit!"

The same referee turned up to handle Moody's clash with future world light-heavy king Jack Delaney. This time he swore at the Welshman and jabbed him in the biceps each time he separated them. After five rounds of this Frank could take no more: one punch sent the hapless official flying into the ropes. It meant another loss on the record and a hefty fine, but the ref had his licence withdrawn, so it was revenge of a sort.

A lengthy rest back in Wales gave hope that a troublesome thumb might have healed, but it went again in the first fight on his return. Even surgery brought only temporary relief and the hand let him down against the fast-rising Tiger Flowers, though Moody admitted the 'Georgia Deacon', who went on to beat Greb twice and win the world title, had carried him in the later rounds and was clearly the better man.

Back in Britain, Todd had been stripped of the Lonsdale Belt for failing to return from the US and defend against Scot Tommy Milligan. When Milligan stopped Guardsman George West the National Sporting Club recognised him as the new champion, with the Empire and European titles as a bonus. Moody decided he should return home and put himself into the mix.

The Albert Hall's new promoters, the International Sports Syndicate, were not prepared to bow the knee to the sport's self-appointed guardians at the NSC. They matched Moody with Todd on February 16, 1927, and billed it for the British title. They also made the fight over 15 rounds, instead of the normal 20, insisting that the shorter distance was quite long enough to discover who was the better man. Frank clearly outpointed the negative Yorkshireman in a forgettable encounter, and Teddy Lewis proclaimed him Britain's top middleweight.

With alternative candidate Milligan tied up by a shot at the new world title-holder, Mickey Walker, Moody turned his attention to the light-heavies and a rematch with Gipsy Daniels, with the Welsh crown at stake even though it took place at the Blackfriars Ring. Frank controlled matters throughout and, as he came out for the final session, heard a bookie so certain of a Moody win that he was offering odds of 33–1 on. He duly strolled through the last round – and then stood in amazement as the referee lifted Daniels's hand.

Gipsy proceeded to dethrone British light-heavy champion Tom Berry, while Moody had to mark time before facing the 37-year-old Berry in Pontypridd, flattening the East Ender inside a minute. Llew had delayed the boxers' entry into the ring until a cloud moved across the sun and then won the toss for corners, condemning Berry to face the glare when it came out again just before the first bell. He was still blinking when Frank hit him and never recovered, suffering a first knockout loss in more than 200 contests.

Milligan was destroyed by Walker, and Moody was talked of as the Yank's next challenger, but Mickey headed for home. Frank opted to stay at light-heavy and halted Yorkshireman Frank Fowler in an official eliminator at Liverpool, the NSC agreeing that he should face Daniels for the title as soon as the club reopened for the new season. But Gipsy rejected the purse on offer and was ordered to hand back the belt, Plymouth's Ted Moore stepping in to face Moody for the now vacant throne on November 28, 1927.

Both were really middles, as underlined when each weighed in without disrobing. Moore, who could already boast three wins over the Pontypridd man, was a good in-fighter, but Frank was happy to indulge him, determined to entertain a crowd that included the Prince of Wales. He picked Moore off repeatedly as the Devonian moved in, taking total control in the later stages, despite a cut caused by a clash of heads. Ted soaked it all up and lasted the 20 rounds, but there was only one winner. Cheering crowds welcomed their hero at Pontypridd station, before the local British Legion band led him to a reception at the New Inn.

A planned meeting with Daniels fell through, so Frank dropped back to middle for a one-round blitz of Milligan before 40,000 at Glasgow's Carntyne racetrack. By then Tommy had lost the NSC-

Frank gets some tuition from trainer Llew 'Bompa' Williams, licensee of the Ruperra

recognised title to fellow-Scot Alex Ireland and Moody immediately agreed to head for Edinburgh's Waverley Market on September 17, 1928, to sort out the matter of supremacy. It looked good for the Welshman when he decked Ireland, a former ABA champion, in the second, but the bell saved Alex and the Leith chemist then kept matters at distance, flicking out his left and using his pace to escape the replies. Ireland was hurt in the 13th, but his trainer, Jack Goodwin, poured a bottle of champagne over his head in the interval and he was sufficiently revived to last the course and win a contentious decision from referee Jack Smith.

Ireland was to lose the belt to the star of the moment, Len Harvey, but not before Moody had faced the Cornishman as a late substitute. A large purse overcame his reluctance to box while out of condition, but he took a battering for six rounds until the referee had seen enough. "In all my life I've never been hit so hard," said Frank.

There was little left. He lost his British light-heavy honour to Yorkshireman Harry Crossley at Holborn on November 25, 1929, in what was was, according to *Boxing*'s headline, "The Worst Belt Fight For Years". A shadow of his former self, Frank still employed the "crouching and springing" style, but without the old fire and vigour. He confessed he could do nothing right – "I knew exactly what I wanted to do, what I ought to do, but just couldn't do them" – and announced his retirement on arriving home.

But nine months later he was persuaded to face old foe Daniels before a 12,000 August Bank Holiday crowd at Cardiff's White City dog track, an appropriate venue for Frank, who bred greyhounds in his spare time. Moody started strongly and finished better to take the decision and win the Welsh

Near the end of his career – Moody draws with Steve McCall at Ninian Park in 1931

light-heavy title as a weight-drained Daniels faded. Naturally, the winner opted to carry on, but his heart was no longer in it and after three more fights he again hung up his gloves.

It was still not the end of the story. In 1935, after nearly four years' inactivity, he was tempted to try again. A couple of quick knockouts raised interest, but he was then flattened by future heavyweight champion Ben Foord.

Moody, now 35, then took on 22-year-old Tommy Farr in what was originally for the Welsh light-heavy belt now held by the Rhondda man, but neither considered the purse sufficient for a title fight. Farr abdicated and the bout went ahead as a non-title contest, ironically for the same money. It ended in a draw, giving Frank a false idea of his remaining ability; the rematch at Greyfriars Hall, on the night of Wales's rugby victory over All Blacks, left no doubt, with Tommy stopping him in four. A seven-round defeat against Southern Area middle champion Frank Hough proved the last straw and Moody realised it was time to say farewell to the ring.

Frank took over the Royal Hotel, Milford Haven, and kept in touch with boxing by promoting a few shows down west. After retiring as a publican in 1959 and returning to Pontypridd, he died, following a stroke, at his sister's home in Thurston Road – the street where it all began nearly 63 years earlier.

GLEN MOODY
(1909–1989)

🥊 **Welsh Middleweight Champion   1931, 1932–33**

🥊 **Welsh Light-Heavyweight Champion   1939–46**

Andy Warhol may have promised everyone their 15 minutes of fame, but Glen doubled it. For a full half-hour the youngest of 13 children from Pontypridd was a guest in sitting-rooms across the country, as the subject of TV's *This is Your Life*.

Other boxers featured on the show, from Muhammad Ali to North Wales-born Alan Rudkin, were chosen principally because of what they had achieved in the ring. Glen Moody's selection owed more to his astonishingly varied career outside the ropes.

There was the BEM he was awarded for his bomb disposal work during World War II, a period which also saw him heavily involved in the evacuation at Dunkirk, one of those he rescued being Swansea's British light-weight champion Ronnie James. There was the youth club he founded in the Australian gold-rush town of Ballarat.

And there was his kindness and compassion, best illustrated when a seven-year-old girl was found sleeping in the gym, wrapped in his over-coat. On learning that she was to be taken into care the next day, Glen and wife Dilys immediately adopted her and raised her as their own.

But he was a pretty useful boxer, too. He may not have matched the collection of belts amassed by big brother Frank, but he did OK for himself, with no fewer than three spells as champion of Wales.

Glen Moody

Given his later activities it was appropriate that his first public appearance came in an exhibition to raise money for hungry children during the 1926 miners' strike. When it came to the serious stuff, Moody soon showed he could handle most of his Welsh contemporaries and did pretty well on his travels, too. But it was on the home front that he had his first title action.

It was an unsuccessful tilt at the Welsh middle crown, however, with holder Jerry Daley's heavier punch and greater stamina enabling him to finish strongly and win an excellent contest. But a year later, on March 30, 1931, Glen lasted the distance better and that made all the difference. He dropped Daley in the fourth, but was under fire himself until the Rhondda man began to tire and, cheered on by a hometown crowd, Moody came through to claim the decision.

Glen gave up the belt after a few months as he turned his attention to the wider world, but a battering from Sunderland's Jack 'Cast Iron' Casey – the Welshman was floored six times on the way to a fourth-round stoppage – dented his dreams and he returned to the domestic scene.

Daley had won the vacant championship with a disqualification victory over Merthyr's Dai Beynon, but once again found Moody too good when they met in Ammanford, almost a year since their last encounter, Glen taking another points verdict.

There was little joy across the border: Casey beat him three times in a row, while he also dropped a decision to Londoner Archie Sexton – whose son, Dave, later managed Chelsea and Manchester United – before being halted in six rounds in a non-title bout by British and Empire middle champion Len Harvey.

Back home things were easier. Moody retained his Welsh crown when Deri boy Billy Thomas was disqualified for a low blow and repeated the victory at the Palais de Danse, Pontypridd, recovering from a slow start and a fourth-round knockdown to batter Thomas in the seventh, cut him in the 11th and dominate down the straight.

When the powers-that-be ordered a third meeting, Glen rejected the purse on offer and found himself stripped of the title. He paid his bills with regular work in England – he lost another four times to Sexton alone – before receiving a further Welsh title opportunity, up at light-heavy.

His superior ringcraft and greater experience proved enough to earn him a narrow decision over former victim Dai 'Farmer' Jones on March 27, 1939, at Haverfordwest, not far from Fishguard, where Glen was now running the Globe Inn. Despite his wartime exploits, he fought regularly and nearly found himself crossing gloves with the great Joe Louis, when the world heavyweight ruler boxed an exhibition at Newport Athletic Club; unfortunately,

The three Moody brothers – from left, Jack, Frank and Glen

a late change of plan saw Louis face a fellow-American, while Moody sparred with another soldier.

Glen was nowhere near full fitness when he faced Vince Hawkins in April 1945, but still floored the future British middleweight boss before losing controversially on points. It marked the end of an era.

Moody gave up the pub and emigrated to Australia in 1955, but homesickness drove him back to Pontypridd four years later and he took over the Criterion, building a gym out the back. He was also a founder-member of the Welsh Ex-Boxers' Association and served on the inaugural committee.

JACK MOODY
(1911–1945)

🥊 Welsh Welterweight Champion   1937–38

The third champion from the Pontypridd family had to leave home to make his name.

Not that he was ever lacking in ability: after taking up boxing at 14, he numbered a young Tommy Farr among his early victims. But it was only after he moved to the Midlands in 1931 to link up with West Bromwich-based Welshman D.W. Davies's expanding stable that he began to capture the attention of a wider audience.

Once he had set up home in the area Moody became eligible for a Midlands title and was matched with Brummie Cal Barton for the welterweight crown in England's second city. At the end of the 15 rounds the referee could not separate them, although most of those in attendance considered the local man had done enough.

Barton made sure when the pair met again five months later, overcoming a slow start to take the decision, Jack finding it difficult to lay an effective glove on his elusive opponent.

Despite his exile, Moody still had designs on honours back in Wales and was soon selected for a welter eliminator against Jack Morgan, one of the Morgans of Tirphil, an even bigger fighting family than the Moodys.

Following reports of his improvement while in England, Moody was a hot favorite when they came together at Bargoed and the early stages showed no reason for his backers to feel unease, particularly as he sent Morgan to the canvas on several occasions. But the Rhymney Valley man changed his tactics and began to box on the retreat. It proved a wise move and he counter-punched his way to the decision.

Jack Moody

There were plans afoot for Jack and Glen to follow big brother Frank's example and try their luck in the States, but they fell through and Jack continued to campaign locally, with mixed fortunes.

He was nevertheless given a shot at Ivor Pickens, a miner from Caerau who had worn the Welsh welter crown for more than three years, repelling all-comers. They met at Cardiff's Greyfriars Hall on October 20, 1937 in a bout which failed to excite the crowd as much as the introduction from the ring of Moody's one-time victim, Tommy Farr, who had just returned from his heroic challenge to Joe Louis. There was little incident until the second, when Pickens landed a swinging left in Jack's groin and was promptly disqualified.

Moody did not enjoy his new prominence for long. His first defence saw him opposed by Cardiffian Johnny Houlston in Newport on July 25, 1938, and despite a confident opening, Jack suffered a badly cut mouth in the second, which clearly disturbed his concentration. Houlston, a former schoolboy star who was still unbeaten as a pro, pulled ahead and, despite a fightback by the holder, emerged a clear winner.

When war broke out, Moody signed up for the forces, but after two years was directed home to work in the mines. It proved a fatal move. Two months after the conflict ended, Jack, still only 34, was killed in a roof fall at the Maritime Colliery.

EDDIE MORGAN
(1892–1937)

Welsh Flyweight Champion 1910

The solitary honour highlighted above does scant justice to one of the best boxers to emerge from the fistic hotbed of Merthyr. With better advice – and, in later years, better health – the former miner from Morgantown might well have had greater achievements to his name.

Had he stayed in Britain, rather than head for the States just as opportunities were opening up for him here, he would probably have worn a Lonsdale Belt. Had his American campaigns not coincided with the 'No Decision' era, he might easily have engaged in full-blown world title fights rather than glorified exhibitions.

And had rheumatism not had its impact on his physical well-being, his period at the top could have been longer.

Back when the 15-year-old Morgan first swapped punches in the booths he would box anywhere, anytime. Most bouts were never recorded, although we know he won a tournament at six stone and, a year or so later was claiming to be Welsh champion at 7st 10lb. When he met his English counterpart, Young Joey Smith, at the Millfield Hotel, Pontypridd, the showdown was billed, with a disdain for the rest of the planet that was typical of the time, as for the world title; in reality, as it was fought over two-minute rounds, it could not even be said to be for the British throne, especially as Eddie was a pound overweight. Smith finished strongly and took the 20-round decision, despite the presence of 'Peerless' Jim Driscoll in the Welshman's corner.

Morgan was back at the Millfield on August 1, 1910, to win recognition as Welsh fly champion by forcing Pentre veteran Jim Southway's cornermen to toss in the towel in the 15th round. Three months

Eddie Morgan, Merthyr's gift to American boxing

later he successfully defended against Jim Dermody, a Swansea Valley-based Irishman, but was never to contest a title again.

By the end of 1911 American promoter Frank Torreyson, via Cardiff referee-journalist Charles Barnett, was trying to get him to tour the States, but Eddie repeatedly refused, claiming he wanted to earn domestic supremacy first. He was considered as a challenger to British fly boss Sid Smith, but, despite his insistence that he could make eight stone, the powers-that-be were rightly sceptical, and he was passed over.

Finally accepting that he was really a bantam, the Merthyr stylist excelled in outscoring black American Young George Pierce at a Liverpool Stadium from which several hundred fans had to be turned away. Those who made it inside were pretty vociferous in support of Morgan and the referee, a Mr Thwaites, on one occasion threatened to stop the bout, such was his distaste for the rowdy behaviour. The ref also received a couple of the wilder punches, apparently without damage, and needed to caution both men in a ferocious encounter said to be among the best seen at the famous venue.

Eddie the dapper man about town

Pierce had drawn with British bantam king Digger Stanley on a previous visit and there was an immediate demand for the champion to risk his crown against Eddie. An official eliminator against Londoner Frank Warner was arranged for Liverpool in August 1912, but instead the Welshman chose this moment finally to answer the calls from across the sea and head to the US.

Morgan made an immediate impression in his three appearances in New York, with future two-weight world champion Johnny Dundee among his opponents, and Liverpool-born manager Jimmy Johnston took out truculent newspaper adverts: "Wanted! A bantamweight or featherweight with enough nerve to step within a 24ft ring with Eddie Morgan." But, as world feather champion Johnny Kilbane headed back to Ohio to be with his pregnant wife, Morgan gave up waiting and sailed back home.

Twice British title matches were made with Stanley; twice they fell through, the first in a mysterious mix-up

Eddie with his first manager, Danny Davies

69

Jimmy Johnston, the 'Boy Bandit', took care of Morgan's affairs in the US

over weight, the second when Eddie pulled out with illness (more likely, an inability to beat the scales) a few days before. Fellow-countryman Bill Beynon took his place and won the belt, but attempts to match the Taibach man with Morgan also came to nothing.

The rheumatism was beginning to hamper him by this stage and his 1913 action was confined to a handful of exhibitions. There was a further handicap when he scalded an arm two days before his competitive comeback against Frenchman Robert Dastillon. The plaster was ripped off during the second of 15 rounds, but, despite being in agony throughout, Eddie hung on to draw.

When he returned to the States in late 1914, leaving behind a Britain at war, he looked a shadow of the man the Yanks had raved about two years earlier. But he had his moments and celebrated Christmas Day by twice flooring Pal Moore – who could boast a win over an admittedly sick Driscoll – and the Philadelphia promoters put him in with the previously elusive Kilbane at the National Athletic Club on January 21, 1915.

It could perhaps be described as a world title fight, in that Eddie would have become champion with a knockout; in reality, it was just another six-round 'No Decision' bout, even if it earned Morgan a generous $1,000 purse and was lauded as one of the best scraps in Philly fight history. The newspapermen whose reports were taken as "results" on such occasions were unreliable guides to what actually took place: after anything remotely close, local journalists would vote for the local man, while correspondents sending accounts to distant papers would tend to see matters differently. So it was with Morgan-Kilbane: the Yanks mostly favoured Johnny, while British publications claimed Eddie as triumphant. When the pair met again the following month, there was a similar split, although Kilbane seemed a clearer winner.

After a brace of close encounters with future world lightweight challenger Rocky Kansas, Morgan headed for home. There were moves to pair him with Porth's newly crowned British feather boss, Llew Edwards, but he could not agree terms and, after just one exhibition at Cardiff Arms Park, crossed the Atlantic again, this time accompanied by wife Violet. He was never to return.

There was plenty of work for him, mostly in 'The City of Brotherly Love', but little success. The newspaper verdicts were now almost always against him and, towards the end, he was unable to hide behind those sometimes questionable judgments, losing four times inside the distance before finally hanging up his gloves.

Settled in Philadelphia with his wife and daughter, June, Eddie collapsed in the street during a heatwave and died in hospital. He was 45.

JERRY O'NEIL
(1909–1997)

🥊 Welsh Flyweight Champion   1930–31

Many boxers come from difficult backgrounds, but few had it as tough as this son of the Merthyr Irish. Born, not merely in the notorious area known as China, but the unforgiving spot they called 'The Arch', he was up against it from the start. When his mother died before his seventh birthday, life became even harder.

With his father, Jeremiah 'Slogger' O'Neil, an unreliable figure, the local Board of Guardians placed him in the Quakers Yard Industrial School, where he also lived. It was no easy number: he had literally to fight for his supper each night, though, as he recalled, "I never went hungry."

His ability with his fists soon earned him a reputation beyond the institution's walls. He won a Welsh schools title in 1920 and added the British in 1925, forming a trio of Merthyr champions alongside Cuthbert Taylor and Tommy Barnes. When the three of them were introduced to a cheering crowd from the stage at Jack Scarrott's booth, the amateur authorities promptly suspended them. Jerry didn't wait to find out how long the ban was; he turned pro.

He made rapid progress and was being named as a title contender while still in his teens, with an eliminator against Cardiff's ringwise Frank Kestrell at Penydarren Park. O'Neil's left jab, already a respected weapon, was constantly in the older man's face and when he landed a following right it split Kestrell's forehead so badly that he had to give up; Jerry was so shocked at the damage he had caused that he burst into tears.

With champion Eddie John relinquishing the belt, his brother, Phineas, was invited to face O'Neil to decide the succession. Despite home advantage at Snow's Pavilion – and an amazing incident in the 11th when Jerry ducked and his foe somersaulted over the top of him, only the ropes preventing serious injury – it was the Rhondda youngster who emerged with a clear-cut decision.

Jerry O'Neil

The three Merthyr youngsters who won British schools titles in 1925, from left: Jerry O'Neil. Tommy Barnes and Cuthbert Taylor

It was a setback, but far from terminal. After a year or two campaigning across England, O'Neil challenged the new Welsh fly king, Freddy Morgan, again at garage owner Ernie Snow's venue near the fountain in Lower High Street, on July 12, 1930. Jerry began strongly, but the Gilfach Goch man took over in the third and dropped him in the fourth, only to land another right while O'Neil's knee was still touching the deck. Despite Morgan's protestations of innocence, no-nonsense referee C.B. Thomas disqualified him and the Merthyr boy was a champion.

With a busy schedule in England – he lost on points to former British fly boss Bert Kirby and future lightweight ruler Dave Crowley among others – O'Neil relinquished his belt.

He tried to regain it nearly three years later, when he met Billy 'Kid' Hughes, a former holder of the unofficial paperweight belt, at Merthyr Drill Hall on March 4, 1933. Despite height and reach advantages, Jerry had problems with Billy's crouching style and the Maesteg-based Rhondda man soon overcame a slow start, a cut caused by a sixth-round head clash adding to O'Neil's problems. That trombone left was still picking up the points, however, and even though Jerry faded late on, the verdict in Hughes's favour still surprised many and prompted noisy dissent from the local fans.

O'Neil boxed on, including a trip to Paris, where he was outpointed by future world champion Valentin Angelmann, but two months later, in April 1934, he was reminded of the dangers of his profession. Knocked out by Mickey McGuire in Newcastle, he was rushed to the city's infirmary in such a precarious state that the Last Rites were read. Paralysed down one side after falling from the ring, it was three weeks before he had recovered enough to be allowed home to Brecon Road, where he was bed-ridden for a further two months.

With a young son and a pregnant wife to feed – and she remained bitter at what she considered a lack of help from the fight fraternity – there was little alternative for O'Neil but to lace up the gloves again.

A few more years in the ring paid a few more bills, but a knockout loss in 1937 to young Brecon prospect Dudley Lewis underlined that Jerry's time had passed. And the blows he took left their mark, as recorded by Merthyr poet Leslie Norris:

"Jerry O'Neill, bobbing his old age

Through a confusion of scattered

Fists all down the High Street"

Appearances were misleading. Despite his unsteady gait, he was still clear of thought, even in his later years in a home in Aberdare. But it is hard to avoid the conclusion that the profession which had enabled him to overcome his early deprivation had exacted a heavy price.

JOHNNY OWEN
(1956–1980)

🏵 **European Bantamweight Champion   1980**

🏵 **Commonwealth Bantamweight Champion   1978–80**

🏵 **British Bantamweight Champion   1977–80**

The new British champion made his way wearily to his room at the luxurious London hotel. Inside he found two of his brothers, whose celebrations had been based on something stronger than the new titleholder's orange juice, spreadeagled across his bed. Johnny Owen, the Lonsdale Belt still strapped around his waist, stretched out on the carpet and went to sleep.

Johnny Owen

There can have been few more unassuming heroes than the miner's son from the Gellideg estate, who carried his shyness as a shield, his experience of the outside world encompassing no greater knowledge of women than of alcohol. There can have been few young men more transformed by the climb up the ring steps. Gandhi put on gloves, Clark Kent became Superman. Except that Superman was immortal, and a Mexican fist was to drive home just how vulnerable was the young man from Merthyr.

That fatal world title encounter with Lupe Pintor inevitably revived the early criticism of his handlers from those who could see no further than the boxer's appearance. His 8st 6lb spread thinly over a 5ft 8in frame, his ribs prominent enough to be counted by the punters in the back row, he looked like a kid, sent out by his mother for a loaf of bread, who had gone in the wrong door. But there was unbelievable strength in that superficially fragile body. An insatiable hunger for training had built a rare stamina, and with it the confidence that he could go flat out from the start and maintain the pace as long as proved necessary.

Each morning at five, watched by ever-present father Dick, he would run some nine miles through the Brecon Beacons (the last stretch of steep slope would be done backwards), returning home to chop enough logs to feed a fur-

Johnny and manager Dai Gardiner relive the moment

nace – and to clear the ashes from the fireplace for his Mam. Each evening, after his shift as a machine setter in a nut and bolt factory, he would head for Merthyr Labour Club to spar in a ramshackle upstairs gym with a series of partners, invariably heavier and invariably exhausted at the end. On his days off from the gym, grudgingly taken, he would merely add a couple of miles to his running.

Johnny Owens – the family name has that final 's' – never lifted a Welsh ABA title, but won on six of the seven occasions he swapped the Courthouse club colours for the red of Wales. When he turned pro in 1976 – dropping

Merthyr welcomes home her conquering hero

Johnny gets the Freedom of the Borough

the 's' and having to be dissuaded from calling himself Siôn Owain out of Nationalist fervour – it was in at the deep end. Cardiffian George Sutton, ranked No 3 in Britain, needed an opponent at Pontypool Leisure Centre. Johnny's licence application was rushed through and the novice's left jab and right cross brought him an upset victory. A repeat performance brought him his first title, the vacant Welsh bantam crown, as he quickly progressed towards a crack at British champion Paddy Maguire. They duly met at the National Sporting Club on November 29, 1977.

Paddy had been through the fistic alphabet. He had travelled the globe, meeting champions from Allotey to Zurlo; Johnny was having only his 10th pro contest. And there was the venue: the mirrors and chandeliers of the Café Royal, with a dinner-jacketed audience including the Duke of Gloucester, were a world away from the workingmen's clubs of the Valleys.

But the Merthyr boy was in charge from the start. He absorbed Maguire's body shots with ease and tied the champion up at close range, while scoring regularly at distance. Paddy was cut and frustrated and at the start of the ninth manager Mickey Duff warned the champion that he would retire him unless he showed an improvement. The proud Ulsterman dug deep into his reserves and won the round, shaking Owen with an overhand right. But the 10th saw the Welshman back in command, and midway through the 11th, with Maguire's eye getting worse, referee Sid Nathan brought an end to his tenure as champion, and to his career.

Johnny acknowledged that it had not been easy. "Maguire made me think," he said. "He was crafty, but I think I was a couple of rounds ahead when it was stopped."

The new titleholder's first defence was at Ebbw Vale, against a fellow-countryman.

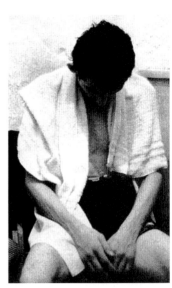
Beaten in the bullring: Owen comes to terms with defeat to Juan Francisco Rodríguez

Wayne Evans was born at Gilfach Goch, but raised at Waterlooville in Hampshire, along with brother Ralph, a flyweight bronze medallist at the Munich Olympics. He had won all 11 bouts, but each contest brought swollen knuckles and there was a feeling of "now or never" about his challenge to Owen.

It was to be "never". The fight had barely started when the right hand went again. Wayne ignored the pain to keep throwing it, but the champion, with his phenomenal workrate, was always on top and the first all-Welsh battle for the British bantam crown soon became one-sided. In the ninth, Evans took a count of eight, and, although he battled back, each punch hurt the thrower more than the recipient. He emerged bravely for the 10th, only to run into a further barrage before half-turning, slumped against the ropes, and referee Jim Brimmell stepped in. The challenger slipped to the canvas and sat, heartbroken, for a full minute before getting up and sportingly applauding his conqueror.

In his dressing-room Wayne wept in agony as the bandages were cut from his damaged hand, revealing a massive swelling, with the middle knuckle invisible beneath a livid bruise. For once Johnny, too, was marked: a slight mouse under the left eye. "Don't put anything on it," he urged his father afterwards. "It shows I'm a fighter."

Owen then stepped up in class to face Paul Ferreri for the vacant Commonwealth throne at Ebbw Vale on November 2, 1978. Southpaw Ferreri, Sicilian-born and Melbourne-raised, had held the title before. His experience vastly outweighed that of the Welshman: Paul had even survived 12 rounds with the fearsome WBC champion, Carlos Zárate, before succumbing on cuts.

The cagey Australian, a renowned counter-puncher, found little opportunity to do anything else against Owen, who rarely let his opponents take the initiative. Gradually the sheer volume of his blows began to overwhelm the visitor, and the almost NSC-like hush of the opening rounds was transformed into a cacophony of song and chanting as the Welshman stormed to a clear victory. "It was like playing at the Arms Park," said Johnny, soon to be elected Welsh Sportsman of the Year.

It was now time to look to Europe. But there were unsuspected pitfalls waiting in the bullring at Almería, where the champion, Juan Francisco Rodríguez, worked as a messenger in the town hall. The Spanish hero was allowed to weigh in some three ounces over the limit, despite protests led by British official Harry Vines. It was a foretaste of events in the ring. When Johnny left the cramped torero's changing-room with its altar on the plaster wall, he was greeted by a bullfight-style band who maintained a constant accompaniment to the action, as though expecting the challenger's Dumbo-size ears to be awarded to a triumphant local idol at the end of the contest.

Merthyr comes to a standstill as Johnny is buried

Their eventual celebration was in little doubt. Despite early success to the body, Owen found it difficult to maintain any rhythm against the Spaniard's negative tactics. Three times the champion was spoken to for holding, he was lectured for a blatant butt in the fifth and finally given a public warning by Italian referee Marcello Bertini in the 12th. For one round he came out with his gloves laced with wintergreen which began to sting the Welshman's eyes. Board Inspector Vines, in his seventies, was manhandled from the ringside by police as he protested to the referee about the goings-on in the Rodríguez corner.

Juan showed some constructive work in the middle rounds and finished strongly, but hardly seemed to have done enough. Nevertheless, the chants of "¡Campeón! ¡Campeón!" which accompanied the last three minutes were not misplaced. The referee and one judge gave the holder the vote by a single point, while the other made it even. It was moonlight robbery.

A year passed before Rodríguez could be persuaded to face Owen again. In the interim Johnny stayed active, a 12th-round retirement victory over Dave Smith keeping his British title intact, one of seven successes in a busy 10-month period. Juan was finally tempted to Ebbw Vale on February 28, 1980. Ironically, he was far more positive than before his own countrymen, and had abandoned the niggling illegalities, but even a below-par Johnny was able to keep his left jab in the Spaniard's face and the visitor was exhausted at the end. This time there was no doubt: all three officials favoured Owen, now a triple champion.

"Gwir Fab o Gymru" says the gravestone at Pant Cemetery; he was indeed a "true son of Wales"

"I'm glad I won, but it wasn't very satisfying," he admitted. "I didn't box well and I got fed up trying to trap him."

There was now constant talk of a meeting with Lupe Pintor, the Mexican who had surprisingly dethroned stablemate Zárate. Manager Dai Gardiner considered his charge was not ready, but his opinion was revised after a superb performance at Wembley to outclass leading challenger John Feeney. His confidence – and that of his manager – fully restored, Johnny now headed for Los Angeles, to tackle Pintor on September 19, 1980. It might as well have been Mexico itself, with the Olympic Auditorium a sea of Spanish, a few rows of travelling Welsh fans providing the only breach in the wall-to-wall support for the champion.

Johnny, entering the ring as ever behind the Welsh flag and his self-mocking skeleton standard, ignored the chants, marching forward and pummelling Pintor on the ropes. The 25-year-old champion, a notoriously slow starter, responded with occasional uppercuts which reminded the Welshman he was in with the best. Owen, however, maintained his single-minded aggression and soon Lupe was open-mouthed and cut over both eyes, bringing his supporters a worrying moment when referee Marty Denkin went to his corner between rounds to check on the wounds.

He was examining the wrong man. The Merthyr boy was bleeding badly from a gash inside his lower lip, but swallowing the blood; he insisted his

The statue that helps keep alive the memory of a champion

seconds stand around him in the corner so that the official could not see the damage. Eventually ring doctor Bernhardt Schwarz took a look, but allowed the fight to continue. Johnny, relieved, maintained the pressure, but Pintor had realised that the Welshman lacked the power to hurt and began to exert his own painful influence.

In the ninth, Johnny walked on to a solid right. A left as he staggered, followed by another right, sent him to the canvas for the first time in his professional life. He rose at three, standing apprehensively for the compulsory eight count, and was under constant fire before the bell came to his rescue. The boundless Owen confidence had suffered a damaging blow, but his courage was never in doubt. Pintor swept on through the 10th, scoring more frequently as the Welshman, uncharacteristically, backed off. The 11th was all Lupe: Johnny threw his share of blows in the toe-to-toe exchanges, but they lacked power, and he was unable to stop the uppercuts raining through a by now flimsy defence. The 12th brought the tragic climax.

A short right felled Owen. He clambered up at four, and nodded, wiping his nose with his gloves, as Mr Denkin asked if he was able to continue. Four blows later came the final right hand: Johnny collapsed like a marionette whose strings had been cut. He was unconscious even before his head hit the canvas with a force that fractured his skull.

Appallingly, the Mexicans cheered the arrival of the stretcher. Some were sufficiently callous as to pick the pockets of the men bearing the sad, still body from the ring. The shell of Johnny Owen was taken to the California Medical Center five blocks away, on a street pathetically named Hope. A three-hour operation to remove a blood clot from his brain did not succeed in pulling him from his coma. It was the Welshman's very fitness that had brought him to disaster; the years of self-sacrifice had given him the stamina which enabled him to carry on when lesser spirits would have conceded defeat. But the postmortem revealed a weakness no amount of training could have repaired: an abnormally thin skull. Today, with compulsory brain scans, Johnny Owen would never have been allowed a licence.

They switched off the life-support machine on November 4, 1980. The Merthyr Matchstick's flame had been extinguished. He was only 24.

LES PICKETT
(1949–)

- Welsh Featherweight Champion 1975–77

- British Featherweight Challenger 1977

Boxing legend has Angelo Dundee tearing Muhammad Ali's glove in order to give the 'Louisville Lip' more time to recover after being floored by Henry Cooper. A similar incident helped British feather king Alan Richardson hang on to his belt against Les Pickett – but it was the Merthyr man's own fault!

Things were nip and tuck after nine rounds at a packed Afan Lido on October 3, 1977, when Pickett indicated a split in Richardson's left mitt. And the three-minute delay while a replacement was produced allowed under-pressure Alan to regroup, finish strongly and sneak Roland Dakin's decision by a single point after one of the best title fights seen in Wales.

"I was already cut and I thought I'd better tell the referee rather than risk making the injury worse," recalls Les, ruefully.

The blond fitter from Cefn Coed had enough problems before the first bell. A training injury confined him to just seven days' sparring, while he needed a pre-fight painkiller after damaging a rib while working out with kid brother Mike, himself a pro. They combined to affect Pickett's timing, but he still maintained a tremendous workrate and Richardson confessed afterwards that it had been "desperately hard".

There were inevitable calls for a rematch, but it was a year to the day before the pair touched gloves again in the same Aberavon ring. By that time Richardson had lost his crown to Nottingham's Dave Needham and the

Les Pickett

10-round contest was merely an eliminator in the search for the new ruler's first challenger.

Despite 12 months' inactivity, Les drew the slick-boxing Yorkshireman – from Fitzwilliam, home of cricket ace Geoff Boycott – into a toe-to-toe encounter and emerged with a two-point margin from Wally Thom, a verdict which prompted the ecstatic victor to throw his arms around the referee's neck in a celebratory hug. Richardson announced his retirement – and his conqueror had only one bout left in his own career.

A rough-house final eliminator against Pat Cowdell, an Olympic bronze medallist who went on to earn two world title shots in the paid ranks, ended with the Midlander a clear winner and firmly on the road to fame and fortune. For Pickett it was the end of a journey which began in a café in Pontmorlais, when a friend pointed out Welsh schoolboy champion Colin Davies across the room.

"I can beat him," insisted Les. "No, you can't," said his mate. So Les went to Eddie Thomas's gym, where Davies trained, and pulled on the gloves for the first time. Moves to Merthyr ABC – and the promised victory over that lad Davies – and the newly formed Courthouse club followed, with Pickett collecting Welsh titles at junior and senior level. But progress in the British ABAs was ended by a decision in favour of future Olympian George Turpin which was so outrageous it prompted an angry letter to *Boxing News* from top promoter Jack Solomons.

After defeat by an East German at the Europeans, Les turned pro, turning down Mickey Duff, at that time second-in-command to the country's other leading figure, Harry Levene, to join Eddie Thomas, with whom Duff had an ongoing feud. It caused a few problems early in his career.

"Duff had a lot of influence and other bantams chose not to fight me," says Pickett. "It meant I was matched tough from the start, fighting bigger men."

That led to a few defeats along the way, but once his contract with Thomas ran out, the phone from London began to ring. One call was to offer him the chance to box at the National Sporting Club on November 10, 1975, as a late replacement against Rhondda boy Alun Trembath for the vacant Welsh feather crown. Les won by a two-round margin on Jim Brimmell's card and, a year later, saw off the challenge of once-beaten Jeff Pritchard in nine rounds at Solihull.

The scrap that earned Pickett his British title bid came at the Albert Hall, when he faced the reigning champion, talented but fragile Vernon Sollas, in an over-the-weight 10-rounder. Floored in the opener, Les gritted his teeth and outlasted the Scot for a stoppage win in the final session.

Alas, it was Richardson, not Pickett, who capitalised on Sollas's vulnerability to dethrone him in his next outing. And Richardson who, complete with replacement glove, denied the Welshman his Lonsdale dream.

TOSH POWELL
(1908–1928)

🥊 Welsh Bantamweight Champion   1927–28

Tragedy haunts boxing like a dark shadow. All who participate, both inside and outside the ropes, are aware of the dangers. But it does not lessen the impact on those occasions, mercifully rare, when a young man pays the ultimate price for his pastime.

Thomas Morgan Powell, known to all and sundry as 'Tosh', was just 20 when the end came, but he had already achieved much in his brief career. His talent caught the eye when he was still at school and, once he moved into the big world, he was quickly on the trail of titles, as if he realised that his time would be limited.

The unassuming youngster – born at Mountain Hare, he spent his childhood at Llwydcoed, after collier father Richard moved to the Cynon Valley – was still a teenager when he challenged Welsh bantam king Johnny Edmunds at Snow's Pavilion in Merthyr on July 8, 1927. The champion from Treharris was struggling at the weight, but that should not detract from Powell's performance in flooring him several times before Johnny retired after 10 rounds.

Within two months, Tosh was defending against the ringwise Nobby Baker at Pontypridd, but for all his experience the Llwynypia miner could not handle Powell's skilful boxing on the retreat and repeatedly found himself walking on to the holder's punches. Baker was never off his feet, but he took a pasting before his seconds pulled him out after the seventh.

Next to challenge was Tom Samuel, trying to avenge fellow-townsman Edmunds and regain

Tosh Powell

IN· LOVING MEMORY

.. OF OUR DEAR ..

Thomas Powell

(TOSH).

4, WESTBOURNE PLACE, MERTHYR TYDFIL.

Who died at Liverpool Stadium, Saturday, 2nd June, 1928,

AGED 20 YEARS.

Interred at Pant Cemetery, Saturday, June 9th.

The family remember a son who died too young

the belt for Treharris. His bid ended in controversy: referee D.W. Davies issued a warning for a low blow in the sixth and, when he sinned again in the following session, Tom was disqualified, despite Powell's pleas that he should continue.

By this time Tosh had established a fierce rivalry with Londoner Billy Housego. The Paddington man first caught the train west in 1927, outpointing Powell at Mountain Ash. When the pair met again at the same venue a few months later, the doors were forced by some of the hundreds locked out and the resultant overcrowding saw the ambulancemen busy treating punters who fainted in the crush. Meanwhile, up in the ring, the fight ended in a draw.

Another meeting was inevitable and it was arranged for Liverpool Stadium on June 2, 1928. It was familiar territory for Tosh, whose three bouts there had been won in a total of five sessions. This time there would be no such triumph. In fact, there was little between them when, with barely a minute left of the 15 rounds, the Welshman was floored in his own corner, striking his head on the boards. He hauled himself to his feet at seven, but staggered back across the ring and the referee waved it off.

Tosh was placed on his stool, but fainted and was carried to the dressing-room, where a doctor had him swiftly transferred to Liverpool Royal Infirmary. He died, his father at his bedside, shortly before six the following evening.

In the aftermath of the tragedy it emerged that Powell had not been training and had wanted to cry off, but the promoters had insisted that he went through with the bout or face possible suspension by the authorities. Stadium director 'Pa' Taylor told the inquest that a substitute had been present if Tosh had pulled out, so there had been no pressure on him, although they did insist on a medical certificate confirming illness; none had been produced, while Powell had been examined by a doctor, who had found him fit to fight.

The post mortem revealed a ruptured blood vessel, probably caused by the fall. The jury duly returned a verdict of accidental death and the fallen hero's body was returned to Wales, where thousands lined the roads to Pant cemetery for the burial, conducted by the Rev. Harry Condie, known as 'The Boxing Preacher'. Among the tributes was a wreath in the shape of a torn harp. It came from Billy Housego.

LLEW PROBERT
(1890–1964)

British Title Challenger 1909

Boxing has often tended to run in families and the Proberts were a fine example, with several of the boys taking up the sport. The most prominent of the fighting sons of Herefordshire-born collier John and his Radnorshire-born wife, Mary, was Llewellyn Francis.

Llew was brought up at various addresses in the centre of Merthyr, the tribe living for a time in Ynysgau, next door to the Patriot Inn. Like so many from that area, he learned to use his fists on the streets before cashing in on his new-found ability on the booths.

He was still in his teens when Joe Shears, from London's East End, visited Merthyr for a 15-rounder with Llew which was billed as for the English (in other words, British) championship at 7st 4lb. Back in 1909, titles were contested at two-pound intervals and, as both men were said to scale less than 7st 2lb, it may have been that honour in dispute. No matter: the bout, at the Welsh National Athletic Club, ended in a draw.

Probert, said to be a fanatical trainer who thought nothing of running from Merthyr to Tredegar and back, impressed some shrewd judges, with none other than Jim Driscoll considering him one of the most promising ringmen in Wales. But the young collier had dreams that would take him well beyond Offa's Dyke in search of fame and fortune.

As well as taking the well-trodden road from Merthyr to Newcastle, Llew headed to London, where he was a popular figure at the Blackfriars Ring before leaving to do his bit in World War I. When peace arrived, he returned

Llew Probert

to Wales, where his successes included a points victory over future two-weight British champion Frank Moody, although the Pontypridd man gained his revenge with a two-round stoppage in a rematch.

Those feet were itching again, however, and in February 1920 Llew boarded the *Orontes* and set sail for Australia. Despite being one of the more successful members of a party of British boxers which included fellow-townsman George Hatto, he did not enjoy his stay Down Under, complaining that the locals were bad sportsmen. (The England cricketers that year, heading for their first 5–0 series defeat, were similarly unhappy.)

After a year or so at home, Probert chose a new destination, opting for South Africa, which he found much more congenial, even though there was little to celebrate in the ring. By the time of his second journey there, he was 35 and, by his own admission, "not getting any younger".

His days as a boxer were numbered and he returned to Merthyr, living at Penyard until his death in Parc Hospital, Bridgend, aged 73.

PRITCH PROBERT
(1888–1928)

🏴 Welsh Featherweight Claimant   1909

The older brother of the well-travelled Llew, Pritchard Morgan Probert confined his adventures to these islands, but still made something of a name for himself.

When he first learned his trade in the booths of the South Wales valleys, there was no group in overall control of the sport. As a result, there were inevitably a string of candidates who claimed to be champions and Pritch began to label himself the featherweight ruler of Wales. He certainly dominated the scene locally, earning special praise for his victory at Merthyr Wonderland on December 4, 1909, in a thriller against Dowlais rival Buff Sullivan.

In a frenetic first round, the taller Sullivan visited the canvas before rising and handing out the same treatment to Probert, who promptly clambered to his feet and floored Buff again. The third of the scheduled 15-rounder brought the climax. Pritch knocked his man through the ropes; Sullivan crawled back into the ring, but was decked once more and, finally, knocked out. Probert was said to weigh nine stone, while the loser, although no exact figure was given, was substantially heavier.

With work hard to come by at home, Probert earned a crust as a commercial traveller, but was also willing to seek pastures new as a pugilist. He spent the summer of 1910 in Gloucester with Sid Russell's booth and the following year headed for the North-East of England, where several Welshmen had tried their luck, and kept on winning.

His first recorded defeat came even further north, in Edinburgh, when he was disqualified against Corporal Tom Evans, bizarrely, for thumbing his nose at the crowd!

There were further defeats away from home, ending any ambitions of chasing one of the recently introduced Lonsdale Belts, and even when he returned to Wales, his dominance was no longer complete.

Pritch headed back to Tyneside, where he married a local girl, Matilda, and raised a family before a tragically early death at Morpeth. He was just 39.

Pritch Probert

BOYO REES
(1912–1955)

Nobody ever called Henry George Rees by his given names. As the smallest, if oldest of the fighting brothers from Abercwmboi – Norman, Ken and Terry all campaigned as pros – he was called 'Boyo' from an early age. It became the handle by which he was known throughout his life.

There was no tradition of boxing in the family, but miner father Will proved something of a latter-day Enzo Calzaghe, guiding his sons throughout their careers. Boyo made his bow at 16, winning and losing in fairly equal measure, but building a reputation as a crowd-pleaser. One battle, against

Ginger Jones in Llanelli, was considered one of the most exciting fights ever seen in West Wales, with the dark, muscular Boyo showing "the undaunted spirit of an Andalusian bull" against the pale, lanky Jones, whose defensive skills were rewarded with a points verdict.

A run of success in 1933 earned Rees an eliminator for the Welsh lightweight title against Pontypridd's Billy Granelly, who had previously outpointed him. This time, however, there was no mistake, Boyo's pressure wearing his man down, and the Granelly corner pulled their charge out after five rounds.

It was nearly a year before the winner had his shot at the crown. Long-serving champion Billy Quinlan had been busy elsewhere, including an unsuccessful challenge to British ruler Harry Mizler, but the pair came together in front of 4,000 fans at the Mountain Ash Pavilion on October 29, 1934, on the first show promoted by Aberdare

Boyo Rees

sportsman Bernard Marcus. The prospect of regular work in his own valley had convinced Rees to turn down offers to settle in the north of England, where he had impressed the locals.

Quinlan, like Granelly, could boast a victory over Rees – though the Cynon Valley boy was ahead when disqualified – but was on a losing streak and Boyo began to take control in the seventh. He shook the Ammanford fighter in the eighth and in the next session landed a solid right to the pit of the stomach. Billy collapsed and rolled out of ring, landing on the floor at the timekeeper's feet. He did not move as referee C.B. Thomas completed the count and was still gasping for air minutes later.

Rees's improvement had been noted by the powers-that-be and he was matched in a British title eliminator against George Daly, but, hampered by a gashed lower lip, he was never able to overcome the speedy Londoner's longer reach and lost a clear-cut decision. Boyo had to lower his sights, but at least he was spared the frustration suffered by Daly, who won two more eliminators and still never boxed for the belt.

Rees saw off ringwise Rhondda miner Nobby Baker in a close encounter which involved little science, both being happy to stand and trade. Baker was cut by a left hook and Boyo was well in front at the finish. His next defence saw a trip to Trealaw to face local Ivor Drew, who had advantages of both height and reach. Rees worked the body, however, and emerged victorious, though several at the Judges' Hall disputed the verdict.

Boyo's reign came to an end in Swansea on January 11, 1937, a cracking scrap with Cardiffian George Reynolds coming to an unsatisfactory conclusion when the champion suffered a split right eyebrow which forced his corner to pull him out in the tenth. It was a setback which wrecked plans for Rees to meet British titleholder Jimmy Walsh.

The year became even worse when the Board suspended him for six months and fined him £10

Boyo has company for his roadwork

following an incident at Pontypool, when Boyo, seconding brother Norman, punched the referee after that gentleman had raised the arm of Norman's rival.

But the authority did not hold a grudge and Rees regained his Welsh crown on April 4, 1938, on home territory at Mountain Ash. This time it was Reynolds who was cut, as early as the opening session, and Boyo was able to dominate, finishing strongly to merit the decision after 15 rounds.

Rees was now more interested in chasing the cash. Twice he faced the exciting Eric Boon, losing in one round at Holborn and in two at Mountain Ash; the Fenland fighter had picked up the Lonsdale Belt in between. The second meeting, at least, was suspicious, with Boyo apparently winking to the crowd as he took the count; it was suggested that Jack Solomons, angling for a world title shot for Boon, had made promises to the Welshman if he didn't rock the boat. In the event, Will, worried that his son might be exploited, did not allow him to join the London-based promoter.

To fulfill that second date with Boon, Rees had turned down a defence against fast-rising Ronnie James. The exasperated Welsh Area Council relieved him of his title.

His job down the pit – by now he was an ostler, looking after the ponies underground – kept him at home during the war, but he boxed only sporadically before hanging up the gloves in 1945.

A decade later he was dead. Found to have a leaking valve in his heart, he was soon unable to work and his old colleagues set up a fund to help him, with Jimmy Wilde as trustee. He never had time to spend the money they raised, falling victim to a cold caught when he defied medical advice to hear his daughter sing in a concert.

DEREK RICHARDS
(1941–)

🥊 Welsh Light-heavyweight Champion   1964–69

Back in the day, when amateur boxing was a regular attraction on television, Britain found a new sporting hero. Billy Walker, a porter from Billingsgate fish market in London's East End, had the looks and the punch, earning himself the nickname of 'The Blond Bomber'. And he first gatecrashed the consciousness of the general public when he flattened a giant American called Cornelius Perry as Britain demolished the Yanks 10–0.

His triumph passed into fight legend – and, as ever with legends, it strayed a little from the truth. Most fans who remember the occasion will point to Walker as the man who completed the whitewash. Not so. The final nail in the American coffin was hammered in by a Merthyr boy with a Midlands accent.

As a heavyweight – super-heavies had yet to be invented – Walker would normally have been the last to box. But his popularity was already such that the BBC asked for the running order to be rearranged to guarantee Billy's appearance in their live slot. As a result, light-middle Derek Richards, from the Rootes club in Coventry, was the Briton faced with the responsibility of closing out a historic whitewash – and the cameras were still rolling as the Beeb extended their broadcast to witness the climax.

In the opposite corner stood a flashy Golden Gloves champion, Roy McMillan, from Toledo, Ohio. With his country's reputation on the line, he came out blazing and gave Richards

Derek Richards

Richards halts Roy McMillan to complete a historic whitewash

plenty of problems in the opening session. But in the second Derek produced three successive rights to the body, McMillan doubled up in pain and the referee waved it off to spark wild celebrations.

Derek, originally from the now demolished Brewery Street, off Brecon Road, was just four when his family moved to the Midlands – Coventry was his mother's home town – and made his first assault on the ABAs via the Midland Counties. But he soon switched to Wales, losing controversially to fellow Merthyr product Johnny Gamble, before winning the middle title in 1962, only to be floored three times by Scouser Alf Matthews in the British final, suffering a broken jaw as he fell to defeat inside two minutes.

It was time to turn pro, managed by Wally Lesley, and trained by two Welsh-speaking exiles, Cockney Johnny Lewis in London and former British heavy king Johnny Williams in the Midlands. Richards's power was evident from the start as he built up a nine-fight winning streak, eight of them via stoppage. Even after suffering his first loss to another Coventry fighter, Jimmy Blanche, Derek gained swift revenge by knocking him out in a rematch.

He had made several appearances in his native land – on one occasion conquering Julius Caesar, though this was a South African version – before facing Cymmer Afan southpaw Stuart Price at Porthcawl's Coney Beach on July 28, 1964, for the vacant Welsh light-heavy belt. It was a bit of a rough house, with both warned frequently for low blows, before Price was pulled out, exhausted, by cornerman Eddie Thomas. Though only 22, Stuart never boxed again.

Derek could hit, but he could also be hit: former amateur star Johnny Ould, British champion Chic Calderwood – in a non-title bout – and unbeaten Italian Giovanni Biancardi all halted him early. But he was still able to retain his Welsh honour with a points victory at the Afan Lido over Cardiffian prospect Eddie Avoth.

It earned him a final eliminator for the British title against Young John McCormack, a rumbustious Dubliner who had taken out British citizenship, with whom Richards had already drawn. This time cuts cost the Welshman and he was stopped in five rounds, but when Calderwood died in a car crash the Board matched them again for the vacant title.

The showdown was repeatedly postponed and, when Derek was again injured, the governing body allowed the Merthyr-trained Avoth to step in and face McCormack. Eddie, too, was badly cut, so it was McCormack in the opposite corner when Richards had his delayed opportunity at the Midlands Sporting Club, Solihull, on November 22, 1967, the first time a British championship had been contested in a private members' club other than the NSC.

Derek had not boxed since their eliminator 13 months earlier, while McCormack had fought five times. It proved a decisive factor, with Richards tentative early on, and John defied disadvantages of height and reach to work his way inside and land with frequency on the Welsh jaw. A gash over Derek's left eye was well controlled by Danny Holland – Henry Cooper's cutman – but it was still one-way traffic until a right-left combination dropped the challenger in the seventh and he took the count, draped over the bottom rope.

There was a brief and painful comeback two years later, Richards looking sluggish and slow against Jamaican Lloyd Walford until cornerman Williams pulled him out after six rounds. Derek got the message and announced his retirement.

FRANCIS ROSSI
(1897–1964)

🐾 Welsh Lightweight Challenger   1921

What is it about Italian musicians settling in Wales and raising boxers? And if harpist Michael Rossi and his Welsh wife did not match Enzo Calzaghe and spawn a world champion, he could at least point to two sons who campaigned at a decent level in the ring.

Francis Bernard never matched his brother in winning a belt, but was generally held to be the better operator and certainly earned the greater fame when he held Jim Driscoll to a draw before 8,000 people crammed into the Mountain Ash Pavilion in 1919. Admittedly, the legend was 38, a full 16 years older than his foe, but the bout underlined that the younger Rossi was not to be taken lightly.

Francis Rossi

From Graig Terrace, near Pontypridd's railway station, Francis worked as a collier's boy at the Maritime Colliery before answering the call and signing up with the Royal Field Artillery, contracting trench fever during a spell in France. As with many other boxers, the Army was generous in allowing Rossi to fit in a fair number of bouts alongside military duties and he was building a solid reputation, both at home and in London, where he became a popular figure at the National Sporting Club.

The draw with Driscoll – followed, sadly, by his father's death less than a fortnight later – was matched when Francis shared the honours with the recently enthroned British feather king, Mike Honeyman, although the title was not at stake.

Domestically, Rossi had missed out on a shot at the Welsh fly belt, coming in a massive eight pounds overweight before outpointing Caerphilly's Arthur Bishop, but he was given a second chance at lightweight against fellow-townsman Jack Joseph at the NSC on March 14, 1921. As with so many important bouts in Francis's life, it ended all square.

Now married and a father, Rossi had to fit his training around work as a taxi driver, but still found time to travel to Marseilles, where a gruesome collection of cuts forced him to quit after nine rounds during which local Lucien Guillot was allegedly the beneficiary of several slow counts.

The search for new horizons next saw Francis board the *Berengaria* with Frank Moody, trainer Llew Williams and manager Billy Ames. It took only one victory – a points success over Harry Carlson in Brockton, Massachusetts, just two months after Rocky Marciano was born there – for the visitor to decide that America was where he wanted to spend the rest of his life.

Young Francis spars with a fledgling Frank Moody in the backyard of the Moody home in Thurston Road

Wife Florence was not convinced. After a six-month visit she headed home to Treforest with three-year-old Bernice and never went back. Francis stayed, starring as a soccer player for Lynn Fosse as well as earning a decent crust from his main sporting activity.

He was still claiming to be the Welsh feather champion in 1926, when it was being contested by others – not that he had ever been universally recognised as such – but it was really only to boost his earning power in the States.

Wales, for Rossi, was in the past. He became a US citizen, married for a second time and died in Massachusetts in 1964.

WALTER ROSSI
(1890–1959)

🏅 **British Bantamweight Contender   1916**

🏅 **Welsh Featherweight Champion   1921**

Most British boxers with transatlantic ambitions tended to build a reputation on home soil before setting sail for the States. Walter's brother, Francis, was one example. But the older Rossi reversed the usual pattern.

Walter Rossi

He left home in the Graig, one of Pontypridd's tougher districts, when barely out of his teens, travelling to the New World to seek his fortune. Within two years he was back, his natural fistic skills honed in that hard environment, in time to fight for his country in World War I. He served in France with the Royal Field Artillery, but still managed to pack in a fair amount of ring action.

A long string of successes in 1915, interrupted only by a disqualification loss, earned Rossi a British title eliminator at bantamweight, taking on Hanley's Tommy Harrison at the National Sporting Club on February 28, 1916, for the right to challenge Joe Fox. Walter had height, weight and strength on his side, but Harrison had the cunning and deserved credit (as *Boxing* put it) "for his skill in holding and getting the other man reproved for the fault". The Welshman was the harder hitter and had Tommy in trouble in the third until he was rescued by the bell; perhaps he spent too much time and effort after that in going for the knockout, for at the end it was the Potteries pugilist whose arm was raised.

Harrison was outscored by Fox when his chance came, but Rossi held the Leeds man to a draw in front of his fervent Yorkshire following, although the belt was not on the line.

Trained by Llew 'Bompa' Williams, licensee of the Ruperra, a Pontypridd hotel which once hosted world heavyweight king Jack Johnson, Walter continued to campaign at a good level. He won and lost against British feather champion Mike Honeyman and came out on top in a series of meetings with ex-bantam boss Bill Beynon, but was halted by one-time world fly ruler Tancy Lee. The Scot was by now fat, bald and 38, but still dominated the lighter Rossi and taught him a few things about in-fighting.

A Welsh title finally came his way – he had claimed the bantam honour without receiving universal recognition – when he took on Billy Morgan, of the Tirphil fighting family, for the featherweight throne at Pontypridd's Mill Field on August 22, 1921. Although Morgan was strong and good at close quarters, Rossi showed more initiative and was the better boxer, clearly meriting the decision.

He never defended, preferring to earn a crust at the likes of Liverpool Stadium and Premierland, in London's East End, where he became a particular favourite. He drew with future European king Harry Mason and then travelled to Paris to face the current incumbent, Eugène Criqui, though the championship was not at stake. It proved disastrous.

There were some brief close-quarter exchanges before Walter found himself on the deck for nine. He had barely risen when a left to the jaw staggered him and a right finished the job inside the first session. Rossi later claimed Criqui had soaked his bandages in plaster-of-paris. Whether or not that was true, war hero Criqui, who won the world crown the following year, certainly had a silver plate in his jaw to repair the damage caused by a German bullet.

It marked the end of Walter's career as a top attraction and he did a bit of refereeing before drifting from the scene. In later years he lived with his sister in Maesycoed, where he died at the age of 69.

TIM SHEEHAN
(1916–1938)

🥊 Welsh Middleweight Challenger   1937

The boy from Caedraw never had the chance to show just how good he could be. Only 21, he had already made one bid for a Welsh title when he suffered a fatal heart attack while sparring.

There had been warnings that the youngster pushed himself – or was pushed – too hard in training. Whatever the truth of that, Sheehan and his two sparmates had done just four two-minute rounds in the dusty Legion gym, opposite the Rising Sun lodging house in Vaughan Street, when he collapsed, never to recover.

The inquest at the Belle Vue Hotel concluded that death was the result of syncope – unconsciousness due to a drop in blood pressure – as a result of an overstrained heart, weakened by pericarditis.

Like so many of that era, Tim had enjoyed little in the way of rest and recuperation during his five-year career, with fights coming thick and fast, particularly on the regular shows at Merthyr Stadium, promoted by George Aris. He had a few outings in Liverpool in 1934 – one on the hallowed turf of Anfield – but mainly stayed close to home.

It's not as though there was a shortage of opposition locally. A particular favourite was Rhymney Valley boy Ginger Dawkins, who faced Sheehan four times without ever having his hand raised. Tim also saw off future Welsh welter king Jack Moody, although the Pontypridd man's retirement was down to a damaged hand.

Tim Sheehan

His tactical astuteness, allied to a fearless attitude, endeared him to the fans and his consistent performances were rewarded with a crack at Welsh middleweight king Dai 'Farmer' Jones at Carmarthen on August 2, 1937. It proved a step too far, too soon.

The Ammanford man had reigned for 18 months, though this was his first defence, and Tim seemed apprehensive as he flicked out a few lefts in the opener, while Jones sought the chance to land his feared right. Then, midway through the second, Dai changed plans, bringing over a vicious left which dropped the surprised Sheehan for a count of eight.

The challenger survived the session, but the third saw him floored no fewer than four times and although the bell rang a split-second into his final visit to the canvas, the referee had seen enough.

There was further pain to come, with a hammering by East Anglian Seaman Jim Lawlor at Briton Ferry. It was to be Sheehan's last fight.

He was preparing to face Norman Rees, brother of Boyo, when he died. The show, at Abertillery, went ahead with Rees facing a substitute, and the Cynon Valley man donated a large portion of his purse money to Tim's widow, who also benefited from a generously patronised collection. It was little consolation for the loss of a husband and father.

TIGER SMITH
(1875–1931)

- World Middleweight Challenger **1907**
- British Heavyweight Challenger **1907**
- British Middleweight Challenger **1908**

Born in Yorkshire, but domiciled in Merthyr's Alma Street, the stocky southpaw whose name was really James Addis met one of the all-time greats at the National Sporting Club on April 22, 1907, in a bout billed as for the world middleweight title.

Tiger Smith

His opponent, the legendary Sam Langford, Canadian-born, but known from his adopted home city as the 'Boston Tar Baby', was certainly worthy of a title shot, even if his colour limited recognition in the US. Smith, on the other hand, seemed to have done little to merit consideration as one of the world's best.

Yet the powers-that-be in Britain at the time even regarded him as a viable contender for the vacant world throne up at heavyweight. The authoritative *Sporting Life* listed him among their four nominees for consideration, along with Philadelphia Jack O'Brien, Tommy Burns – who eventually won it – and Londoner Gunner Moir.

Smith was, it's true, the Army champion and that, coupled with a record of heroism in the Boer War, may have been enough to persuade the patriotic 'Peggy' Bettinson and his cronies at the NSC that the 'Tiger' deserved to rank highly.

That theory was blown apart when Moir, some 20lb heavier, destroyed him in just over two minutes. The contest, for the English (that is, British) heavy title, was filmed, apparently showing the former Hussar to be "a third-rater", but the general public were never allowed to witness it because the future kings, Edward VIII and George VI, could be seen at ringside.

Despite that humiliation, two months later Smith was crossing gloves with Langford, who was, at least, a similar size. It, too, ended disastrously for the Merthyr man, who was counted out less than a minute into the fourth session. Even his backers admitted he had been outclassed, with little idea of defence.

This 'Tiger' could bite, though, and after despatching Londoner Charlie Allum inside a round and Brummie Jack Costello in rather longer, he was again challenging all and sundry. He spent some time in Paris, although one contest at the casino there was cancelled after an official ran off with the takings.

But Smith did get one more chance at a belt (or even two) when he faced Penygraig's Tom Thomas at the NSC for the Welsh and English titles at 11st 4lb. 'Tom Farmer' knocked him out in four and when he was also flattened by Dave Peters, another Rhondda man, it spelled the end of his claims to championship honours.

Ironically, having served throughout the Boer War without a scratch, he had much of his scalp removed in a roof fall at Deri Colliery, which effectively ended his career. He nevertheless was accepted back into the services in World War I, eventually becoming a sergeant-major in the fledgling RAF.

He was once again to find peacetime life a lot more dangerous, losing three fingers in an accident at Dowlais steelworks. He was also a licensee for several years, before dying at home in Castle Street.

CUTHBERT TAYLOR
(1909–1977)

🥊 **Olympic Representative   1928**

🥊 **Welsh Bantamweight Champion   1929–30**

If ever there was a case of someone being born at the wrong time it was Cuthbert. Today he would have a Lonsdale Belt in his cabinet and be up there in the mix for world titles. He was good enough to achieve such things in his own era. But his skin was, as his father scornfully put it, "just a little bit brown".

For the men who mattered that was enough to bar him from the domestic game's top prizes. Even the Welsh championship he claimed was unofficial; once the Board of Control was up and running Cuthbert was told he could not be considered.

Cuthbert Taylor

The Georgetown-born youngster had boxing in his blood: his Liverpudlian father, Charlie, had more than 200 fights before becoming a deacon at Salem Chapel. His son learned the basics at the National Sporting Club – though this one was in a loft above Hazard's pop factory. But he was soon to face his first clash with the authorities.

When he captured a British Schools title someone told the English ABA that he worked on a milk round. He had to produce proof that he was indeed still a pupil at Twynyrodyn.

At least Taylor's skin did not seem to be a factor and, after claiming British ABA honours in 1928, he was selected for the Olympics in Amsterdam. Competing at flyweight, the teenager defeated an Argentinian before losing on points to the Frenchman who went on to win silver. His amateur career also included victory at the Tailteann Games in Dublin, where his trophy was handed over by world heavyweight boss Gene Tunney.

Turning pro – and making his debut at the real National Sporting Club – he soon laid down a marker by halting reigning Welsh fly champ Eddie John. When he returned to Covent Garden to face Brummie Bert Kirby in April 1929, the NSC hinted heavily that the winner would challenge British fly champ Johnny Hill; presumably the gentry had not yet noticed that Cuthbert failed to meet their standards of racial purity. In the event Kirby won the decision.

But there was greater joy on home soil. He was on top from the start against Danny Dando at Pontypridd on July 29, 1929, cutting his Merthyr rival on the cheek and totally dominating for the full 15 rounds to earn himself general recognition as Wales's top bantamweight.

Taylor returned to the Palais de Danse just five weeks later to face former fly king Phineas John, who was a big outsider despite a previous victory over the champion. The Rhondda man's elusiveness and success on the counter ruffled

Cuthbert and father Charlie about to leave for a fight in Paris

Cuthbert, who became wild and, when he did land one of his heavier blows, failed to follow up. Even when he decked Phineas in the 12th, the challenger recovered to control the final sessions and get the decision.

But the bout had been made at 8st 7lb, one pound over the division limit, so Taylor was still considered the champion and, as such, was matched with Irishman Packey McFarland at the NSC's temporary base at Holborn, with strong hints that the winner would box for the Lonsdale Belt. Cuthbert's dream was dashed when referee Eugene Corri disqualified him for holding, a decision so harsh that even the club's well-mannered members "gently booed" the official.

Taylor avenged that loss with a clear-cut points win over McFarland, but it took place at Hoxton Baths, so the NSC barely noticed it happened. There was no more talk of British title opportunities.

Cuthbert was coming under pressure to defend his Welsh crown against Stan Jehu, the son of a mountain fighter from Maesteg, who had beaten Dando in an eliminator. The pair met in Pontypridd on February 24, 1930, and Taylor lost his title because of a costly miscalculation. Believing himself to be well ahead, the Merthyr man contented himself with keeping a light left flicking into Jehu's face. But Stan had been scoring to the body and keeping matters

Cuthbert loosens up on the punchball

close on the card of referee F.R. Hill. When the challenger took the last three sessions against a tiring Taylor it was enough to clinch victory.

A popular figure in France, Cuthbert went the distance with former world fly champion Émile 'Spider' Pladner in Paris and came near to beating an actual title-holder when he faced American Freddie Miller, who ruled the planet's featherweights, losing on points at Liverpool Stadium.

Between those contests, Taylor had his last bid for domestic honours, a return with Jehu, but the Llynfi Valley man overcame a slow start to have Cuthbert on the verge of being stopped in the 13th, though he survived to lose on points.

Taylor moved up to feather and, with his colour now an issue, the Welsh Board asked their London masters to rule on his eligibility for a shot at British champion Nel Tarleton, given that Larry Gains, the black Canadian, had been allowed to contest the Commonwealth heavy belt. The Board replied that Gains, as his country's titleholder, could not be refused; the British throne, however, could only be occupied by a white man.

It was a ruling which also denied him the opportunity to tackle Ginger Jones for the Welsh nine-stone title, so they met for a £50 sidestake before a packed house of 3,000 at Merthyr Stadium, with an estimated 4,000 turned away and hundreds waiting outside for the result. Referee Will Bevan's verdict in favour of Taylor created much dissent; the fight had been full of skill, but it was claimed that Jones's effective counterpunching had won it. The Jones camp claimed they immediately wanted a rematch, with the sidestake up to £100 or more, but Cuthbert could not be tempted.

Taylor boxed on, winning more than he lost, until the end of World War II, in which he served in the Navy as a PTI. His retirement was bedevilled by arthritis in his knees – aggravated by a crash in a Hoover lorry – and he died at home in Vaynor, aged 67.

DAN THOMAS
(1828–1910)

🥊 Bare-Knuckle Champion   1850s

When they buried the 81-year-old chapel deacon, ministers queued up to pay tribute to a former colliery owner and philanthropist, known for his piety and his generosity to Dr Barnardo's and other charities.

What was not mentioned in the service at Glyntaff cemetery was the other life of the man once known throughout Britain as 'Dan Pontypridd' or 'Dan yr Union'. For the respected pillar of the community they laid to rest had been one of the outstanding pugilists of his era.

Brought up in Pwllgwaun, Thomas was a stocky 5ft 5in, with a body that was described as "of the good old stone-wall type". He soon discovered a talent for fighting which brought him to local prominence, culminating in a repeat victory against the much bigger Evan Williams over 50 rounds before a huge crowd at Machen.

Dan tasted defeat on a return to Monmouthshire on February 5, 1856, to face a Brummie known as Duck Ingram. After an hour's brutal beating, Thomas's backer, English champion Johnny Walker, threw in the towel.

The Welshman had neglected his training for that bout, but was in top condition two years later when he made his first appearance in a London ring, against Jack Brookes, from Norwich, a man who had beaten Dan's conqueror, Ingram. The bout was made at 8st 6lb, although Thomas was barely eight stone, yet his improved fitness allowed him to demonstrate his superior technique and, after 55 rounds, he emerged victorious to be regarded by the Fancy as the best around among the lighter men.

An American, Charlie Lynch, had been considered unbeatable, but Dan beat him. Then he faced Brighton's Bill Gilham for £100 a side and Thomas cashed in by knocking his man out with what a witness described, with a certain understatement, as "a fairly hard blow".

After returning to Wales, Dan slipped off the radar of the London-based chroniclers until what seems to have been his last fight, against Midlander Joe Nolan at Aldermaston on April 8, 1862. Among the ringsiders was the American, John Camel Heenan,

Dan Thomas

two years after his legendary showdown with Tom Sayers. The 'Benicia Boy' had postponed a trip to Paris in order to attend, which gives some idea of Thomas's eminence in the prize ring.

Heenan and his cohorts were to have a frustrating time, however. After just three rounds the police intervened and there was a two-hour delay before it was deemed safe to resume hostilities. The pair battled away for another 20 sessions before the Peelers returned, this time ending the encounter for good.

Outside the roped square, Thomas became a successful landlord at a series of Cardiff pubs, but after shut-tap he spent hours poring over a book of sermons. In due course, he turned his back on punches and pints and was baptised at Libanus, a Welsh-medium chapel at Treforest.

He invested his earnings in an Ogmore Vale coal mine and amassed a small fortune, setting up home in Porthcawl.

Dan's rejection of his former self was total. He burned the ornate belt he had been awarded following the Nolan contest and a gold watch he had won earlier met the same fate "so that my children should never see them and be tempted to take any delight in such a life".

The star of the prize ring who became a pillar of society

Even a young Freddie Welsh was on the receiving end when he met the former bare-knuckle bruiser in his last years. "This fighting," said the old man. "It doesn't pay. Give it up, my boy."

EDDIE THOMAS
(1926–1997)

- European Welterweight Champion **1951**

- Empire Welterweight Champion **1951**

- British Welterweight Champion **1949–51**

- Welsh Welterweight Champion **1948–49**

The foundries of Merthyr once produced iron and steel to span the world. The days of industrial glory are long gone, but the homely valley town still forges a very special breed of men, none of them more proud of his birthplace than Eddie Thomas. It was a mutual respect. If Eddie regarded Merthyr as somewhere God made when He'd finished practising on Eden, his fellow-townsmen thought highly enough of him to have elected him to the local council. As an Independent, of course.

Thomas had come a long way from the little terraced cottage in Upper Colliers Row where he was born. But while his luxurious detached house at Penydarren was evidence of the material success of the journey, its proximity to his childhood haunts testified that on all his ventures into the wider world he carried a return ticket. And the whole drama was played out before the constant backdrop of the pit; from tyro to triple champion, from choirboy to councillor, he never stopped working underground.

The family had always known how to use their fists. Grandfather John Thomas, known as 'Shoni Q', was a deacon at Bethesda Chapel and once engaged in a two-hour scrap with Jim Fury, head of a gipsy band who were camping alongside the canal. Just to add to the combative bloodline, John married a daughter of the fighting Vaughan family.

Eddie was barely 14 when he followed his father to the Cwmdu drift, earning 16s 6d (82 1/2p) a week. That was two years before he laced on a competitive glove, though in the

Eddie Thomas

The old gym in Penydarren – behind the first-floor bay window of the building near the cars – produced a string of champions

ring, as in the mine, he learned fast, under the watchful eye of Ephraim Hamer. His second contest brought a Welsh junior title, though his religious parents knew nothing of it.

"They wanted me to concentrate on my studies," he recalled. "They thought I was going to night school. I had to hide my shorts and boxing shoes underneath an overcoat, even though it was summer. I was sweltering!"

In his fifth bout he added the British junior prize, before a senior amateur career which culminated in the ABA lightweight crown in 1946. A few weeks later Eddie, with the backing, now, of his father, who had himself been handy with his fists, turned pro with the experienced Sam Burns, who, as an employee of Jack Solomons, guaranteed influence in high places.

With a record blemished only by a cuts loss to Yrjö Piitulainen, 'The Crooning Finn', the Merthyr miner soon earned a British title eliminator at Harringay against Welsh champion Gwyn Williams. Blond Gwyn had been born at Pontycymmer nine years before his ex-pro father Billy moved the family to Oxford to run a chicken farm. There was nothing chicken about Gwyn – a paratroop instructor during the war, he had flown over Arnhem during the airborne landings – but it was only after his father accused him of being yellow that he became a pro fighter. He proved no mean operator. Williams's tight defence was impenetrable and in a classic contest Gwyn took a close, but undisputed verdict.

Eddie was desperate for revenge, but first he was given a non-title bout with veteran champion Ernie Roderick, on the White City bill that saw Freddie Mills win the world light-heavyweight crown from American Gus Lesnevich. Ernie was 34 and had worn the Lonsdale Belt for more than nine years, but all his experience counted for nothing against the confident Welshman. Despite a thumb injury caused when he trapped a hand in the door of a colliery tram, Thomas must have landed at least two blows for every one by Roderick, who showed typical Scouse generosity with a slap on the back as the youngster's arm was raised.

Then came Williams again, and this time Eddie took control in the later stages to clinch a 12-round decision and with it the Welsh title.

The following year, 1949, brought Thomas his best scalp to date. Billy Graham, a rough, tough specimen from New York's East Side, had lost only three of his 86 fights and, at 25, was in his prime. But Eddie jabbed his way to a comfortable victory, leaving Billy with a large egg over his left eye. The jubilation was shadowed with worry over Eddie's left hand. He was sidelined for three months, receiving manipulative treatment from a London specialist to ease a problem he now confessed had bothered him for the past year.

His reappearance was in a British title eliminator at Liverpool Stadium against Stan Hawthorne, and those fragile fists were firm enough to stop the man from North Shields in the third. Roderick had by now lost his throne to another of Eddie's early victims, Henry Hall, but still entertained hopes of reclaiming it. He and Eddie met again on a September night at Harringay. A sharp right sent Roderick to the canvas in the opening minute, but the old-timer

Throughout his boxing career and beyond, Eddie worked underground

recovered to win the early rounds. Thomas, learning to combat Ernie's feints and dummies, came back to dominate an all-action last quarter and edge the decision.

So it was Thomas who took on Hall, at Harringay on November 15, 1949. The 27-year-old blacksmith's striker from Sheffield came into the ring having lost his three previous contests; Eddie, four years younger, had won 11 on the trot. If Henry's confidence was therefore suspect, it was further diminished in the early rounds. Hall landed his pet right hook as soon as the first minute, and it had no apparent effect; then Eddie buckled Henry's knees in the second round with a vicious right to the body. The champion survived, but it was apparent that, barring accidents, the title was about to have a new owner.

Yet the 13th round could so easily have proved disastrous for the Merthyr boy. He caught Hall on the hip with a powerful right, which sent the holder to the deck in agony. Had he stayed there, referee Moss Deyong must have disqualified Thomas. But the brave champion pulled himself upright before the count could reach 10, Eddie escaped with a stern warning and duly collected his points verdict. And he had enough breath left to take the ring mic and serenade the assembled gathering with *Bless This House*, before giving journalists the classic post-fight quote: "Tell Mam I'll be home for tea."

Mam was in fact one of the few people in Merthyr who hadn't listened to the radio commentary. She couldn't face it. But the rest of Upper Colliers Row took to the streets, flashlights in hand, to drape bunting over the railway bridge and the hedges ready for the triumphal homecoming.

Jack Solomons began wheeling and dealing in a bid to entice world champion Sugar Ray Robinson to Britain, but the fight never materialised, and Thomas had to look closer to home for his next action. On September 13, 1950, he faced Cliff Curvis at Swansea's St Helens rugby ground in the first British title fight between two Welshmen in Wales. The 22-year-old southpaw had failed in eliminators at feather and lightweight before outpointing Gwyn Williams to secure a crack at the 10st 7lb crown.

Curvis, faster of hand and foot, started well, with his flicking right rarely

out of the champion's face, and his left landed in the fourth with such effect that Thomas's jaw was dislocated and had to be reset in the corner so that he could continue. Eddie began to score to the body and Cliff was warned for hanging on after one such assault. Another, in the sixth, sent him down, grimacing with pain and complaining that the blow was illegal. Referee Jack Hart gestured that Curvis had risen on his toes in a bid to avoid the punch, so if it strayed below the belt it was his own fault.

Tempers became somewhat frayed after that, and Mr Hart had to separate the pair when they tried to continue discussions after the bell to end the eighth. Both men were cut and Thomas, the more troubled by the blood, struggled to land a telling punch until the final minute of the contest. Then a thunderous right to the chin had Curvis wobbling and,

The sculptor has captured the ramrod straightness of the Thomas left lead

although he managed to remain vertical, he was still in difficulty at the gong. Mr Hart had no hesitation in lifting Eddie's arm, but Curvis's hometown crowd made known their discontent.

Thomas completed the year in less than distinguished fashion, scraping a draw with Frenchman Titi Clavel and then overturning his car. But his second major title was on the horizon. The Empire welterweight crown had lain dormant since Tommy Milligan relinquished it in 1924, but sup-

Eddie (right) defeats Pat Patrick in Johannesburg to add the Empire title to his collection

porters of a young South African called Pat Patrick were keen for its revival and the local hero was paired with Thomas at Johannesburg's Wembley Stadium on January 27, 1951. The flight out was a bit hairy, but the contest itself brought Eddie fewer alarms. Watched by 15,000 in pouring rain, his science was far too complete for the boy from Germiston, and matters were brought to a satisfactory conclusion in the 13th with a jolting right cross and a perfectly timed left hook.

Within a month Thomas had added a third honour. Michele Palermo, a 39-year-old farmer from Caserta, near Naples, had been Italian champion five times over an 18-year period, finally winning Continental honours the previous July, and had been stopped only once in 117 pro fights. Yet within 10 seconds of the start of their meeting, at Carmarthen's Market Hall on February 19, 1951, he was on the floor from a shock left hook. The champion's stamina was bottomless, however, and although he visited the canvas again in the last round, he deserved the dignity of losing his title on his feet.

Eddie wore the triple crown for only four months, thanks to a fellow miner from Fouquières-les-Lens in North-East France, 24-year-old Charles Humez. The butcher's son had already disposed of two Welshmen, stopping Gwyn Williams in three rounds and outpointing Cliff Curvis, the latter in the very Coney Beach arena in which he met Thomas. With Robinson being urged to relinquish his welter belt, having just become middleweight champion, the

Eddie stands over fallen challenger Wally Thom, but it was the Birkenhead man who came out on top

Board of Control, backed by the European authorities, decided to recognise the Thomas–Humez bout as a final eliminator for a vacant world title.

There were suggestions that the prospect of such greatness overawed the Merthyr man. Whatever the reason, little of his usual skill was on view for the 10,000 spectators and Humez took an emphatic decision. Eddie ended the evening cut on the forehead and over both eyes, his international aspirations equally battered. Domestically, too, the great days were drawing to a close.

Nemesis was approaching in the shape of Wally Thom, a 25-year-old southpaw from Birkenhead, who had actually won a Welsh ABA title while in the Army. Thom had been beaten just once, on cuts, in 23 paid outings. Eddie was always a slow starter, and at Harringay on October 16, 1951, it proved fatal. The red-haired challenger was allowed to construct a solid points lead, despite sporadic rights from Thomas which caused Wally to touch down briefly in the second and fourth rounds. Although the Merseysider shipped a fair amount of punishment in the later stages, his gameness and determination enabled him to survive, exhausted, but the new champion of Britain and the Empire. The hair's-breadth decision left Eddie heartbroken.

"It took a lot out of me to make the weight," he lamented. " But I felt myself coming strongly after midway. I thought there wasn't very much in it."

A fine collection of injuries, notably a bad knee sustained playing soccer, delayed a comeback. Eventually a cartilage had to be removed and in all 18 months had passed when he stepped between the ropes again. Three wins earned him a match with Ulster titleholder Bunty Adamson in an eliminator for his old crown, and the two Celts met in the passionate surroundings of the King's Hall, Belfast. Once again Thomas, hampered by a touch of rheumatism, was slow getting into the fight, and although he was on top at the end referee Eugene Henderson called it a draw.

When the two were rematched at the same venue, the more skilful former champion again allowed the 23-year-old from Banbridge to cut out the work and this time Scottish official Peter Muir was able to find a winner – and it wasn't Thomas. A great career was near its close, and in December 1954 he took what proved his final bow. There were three rounds of exquisite boxing before the Welshman began to tire, and the strength of a young Channel Islander named Ron Duncombe gave him a points victory. For Eddie, it was enough. He announced his retirement.

Of course, this was not a journey to oblivion: indeed, when the Welsh Area Council celebrated their half-century in 1980 Eddie was honoured as the man who had done most for the sport in Wales during that period. The master boxer proved an adept teacher, guiding Howard Winstone and Scot Ken Buchanan to world titles and Colin Jones to the brink of equalling their feat. As a cutman par excellence, he ministered to the fragile features of such as Henry Cooper. As a promoter, he was a one-man life-support system for professional boxing in South Wales at a time when it flirted with extinction.

As a citizen, he played a heroic role in the recovery of bodies after the tragedy of Aberfan and later took up the cudgels for bereaved families affected by subsidence at Cefn cemetery, above his beloved town.

There was another fight, too, against cancer. For a while it seemed as if Thomas had won through and his fellow-townspeople showed their relief and pride by granting him the Freedom of the Borough in 1992. An even greater honour followed, when he became Mayor in 1994 – "It's better than winning a world title," he insisted – but that turned sour when he was forced to resign as financial problems brought him to the brink of bankruptcy.

The cancer, too, came back, finally claiming its victim on June 2, 1997. His funeral at Tabernacle Chapel was nevertheless a joyous occasion, gusts of laughter filling the hall as those who knew him best told their stories. The man and his environment were inseparable. In fact, his epitaph could be deciphered in the M.B.E. he was awarded in 1984: it really stands for "Merthyr Boy, Eddie".

His Worship the Mayor

HUGHIE THOMAS
(1928–2003)

🥊 Welsh Bantamweight Champion   1952–53

I t is only natural that a younger brother should be proud when his elder sibling achieves success. And Hughie was. It was just that when you are hoping to follow him into the same field of endeavour, it can be difficult to escape the large shadow.

Named Urias, after his father, it was no surprise when the Old Testament moniker became something more manageable for his ring activities. The newly labelled Hughie began with the Cardiff-based Melingriffith ABC and reached the Welsh ABA flyweight final in 1947 (a year after Eddie was a British amateur king), only to lose to city boy Jackie Sutton.

A switch to Merthyr Youth for the next season, coupled with a step up to bantam, helped him go that extra yard to the title. The following year he reached the British final of the National Coal Board championships, in those days a major competition, before turning pro in 1950.

Thomas began with a string of victories, interrupted only by a points defeat on a trip to Lincolnshire, and was soon matched in an eliminator for the Welsh bantam crown. In the other corner was a farm boy from the outskirts of Pontypool, Roy Ball, who had nine years' extra experience in the paid ranks. No matter to Hughie; he knocked him out in six rounds.

The champion, Thomas's old amateur rival, Jackie Sutton, gave up the title to campaign at featherweight, and the Merthyr man found himself facing Ball again, on May 26, 1952, at the Market Hall, Abergavenny, to fill the vacancy. Despite his previous triumph, it was not to be easy.

Even before the first bell, Hughie needed to sweat off 12 ounces to make the weight. Then, in the third round, he

Hughie Thomas

Hughie greets rival Roy Ball before their Welsh title clash, with promoter Albert Davies on the right

damaged a knuckle on his right hand. But his wide repertoire of punches still proved too much for the game Ball, whose corner called the referee over after eight painful sessions to announce his retirement.

The new ruler was never able to cash in on his achievement. The injured knuckle failed to heal properly and had to be broken again and re-set, keeping him out of the ring for more than a year. And the enforced idleness meant any thoughts of staying at bantam had to be abandoned, forcing Thomas to hand back the belt without defending it.

For his first outing at feather, Hughie faced Tiryberth's reigning Welsh monarch, Haydn Jones, at Ninian Park, taking the decision over eight rounds to earn a rematch for the championship on October 26, 1953. Unfortunately, it resulted in what the *Boxing News* report described as "one of the dreariest contests ever witnessed at Sophia Gardens". And, as if that wasn't bad enough, Jones took the decision.

Recurrent stomach problems meant Thomas had only one more bout. He was knocked out in five by Croydon's Malcolm Ames and called it a career.

He became assistant to brother Eddie in the old snooker hall in Penydarren, later known as 'The Sweat Box', taking responsibility for organising the training schedules, and many of the gym's boxers benefited from Hughie's gifts as a motivator.

JASON THOMAS
(1976–)

🥊 British Bantamweight Contender   1999

It would have been a bit daunting for any young boxer. As he glanced across the ring at his highly touted Puerto Rican opponent, he noticed a couple of familiar faces in the corner: Félix Trinidad, already five years into his reign as IBF welterweight champion, and Wilfredo Vásquez, a week ago the WBA feather king, who had been stopped by Naseem Hamed earlier on the same Manchester card.

Jason Thomas

But the factory worker from Dowlais focussed on Héctor Orozco, the only one of them allowed in the ring once the bell had rung. And he held his own to be rewarded with a draw after four highly competitive rounds.

Thomas may not have had such immediately recognisable faces in his own corner, but Gareth Donovan had done a pretty good job in developing the youngster from his first steps inside the door of the gym at Gellifaelog and later at Penydarren and the Merthyr Ex-Servicemen's club. A clutch of junior awards was topped by a bronze medal from the European Under-16 championships, where he was outpointed by the Hungarian later to be honoured as the best boxer in the tournament.

Word of this promising talent had reached the ear of Irish guru Brendan Ingle, who invited Jason and big brother Chris to join him at his famous Wincobank gym in Sheffield. After nine months there, the pair opted to try Florida, but a year later, Jason turned down offers of a pro contract to return home and link up with Dai Gardiner.

As a result the younger Thomas made his paid bow in the less exotic surroundings of the STAR Centre in Cardiff's Splott. A points decision over West Walian Henry Jones gave the 19-year-old a satisfactory introduction, but his next five fights ended in defeat. His conquerors did include future titleholders Noel Wilders and Jason Booth, but also former victim Jones. It did not bode well.

Yet an impressive knockout of previously unbeaten Ulsterman Colin Moffett heralded a gradual improvement in Jason's results, including a win over future British fly king Keith Knox and the draw with Señor Orozco. His losses were against world-class campaigners such as Peter Culshaw and Michael Alldis and the Board recognised the fact by naming him to face former foe Wilders in an official British bantam eliminator in Halifax on February 6, 1999.

The unbeaten Yorkshireman pleased his home fans by dominating throughout, picking off his fellow-southpaw with ease, despite Thomas's determined attempts to work inside. Referee Terry O'Connor gave the Welshman only two rounds, with one even, and Wilders moved on to capture domestic and European belts.

For Jason, it was as far as he would go. There were only two wins and one draw in his next 16 contests – one victory came over Swedish-Rwandan Frankie de Milo, who reversed it in a rematch for the vacant British Masters super-bantam strap – and after a first-round loss to Mauritian debutant Riaz Durgahed, the Merthyr man called it a day.

Five years later, in 2009, Thomas returned to the ring under the guidance of Brian Coleman, but suffered half a dozen points losses and a 77-second battering by former amateur ace Stephen Smith, now the Commonwealth champion.

His lack of success led the Welsh Area Council to veto a proposed 2011 meeting with Cefn Fforest youngster Robbie Turley for the vacant Welsh super-bantam title. But, despite the disappointment, Jason, who has a day job at the DW Sports gym off Swansea Road, dismisses any suggestion of retirement.

BILLY VIVIAN
(1955–)

🥊 Welsh Light-Welterweight Champion 1978–82

Originally from Cefn Hengoed, Billy had already amassed a sizeable collection of trophies and titles before moving to Merthyr as a 15-year-old when his parents took over the Swansea Road Club. A multiple champion at junior level, he matched that by claiming the Welsh ABA featherweight crown as a senior, only a Celtic boycott of the British ABAs preventing him performing on a wider stage.

He took a few years off before joining the pros. Now married and living on the Gurnos, Vivian nevertheless returned to his old stamping ground for a manager, signing with Dai Gardiner, who had trained him in his last years in the vest and headguard.

With few promotions in Wales at the time, it meant a lot of travelling, though this did not seem to affect Billy's progress, demonstrated early on with a points victory over previously unbeaten Scot Willie Booth. But having to face local heroes in their own backyards was always problematic and he suffered his first loss when future European champion Colin Power halted him in four rounds in London's East End.

Trips to the Smoke brought further setbacks, with a points loss to Ray Cattouse, who went on to win a British title, and a first-round knockout by Cornelius Boza-Edwards, who was to wear the WBC super-feather belt. They began a sequence of seven successive defeats, including a Welsh lightweight challenge to Merthyr rival Johnny Wall at Ebbw Vale, which saw the holder's go-forward style take the honours over Vivian's neater boxing.

There were some classy characters among his conquerors, however, none more than legendary Scots southpaw Jim Watt, who was European ruler when 'Billy Viv' lasted the full eight rounds with him in a non-title encounter. Future IBF super-feather boss Barry Michael, an Aussie who was spending a period with the Eddie Thomas camp, was another who had to settle for points.

There was something to celebrate along the way, too, when the newly established light-welter division offered him a chance to put his own name on the roster of champions. Vivian took on Llantwit Major's Dil Collins at the

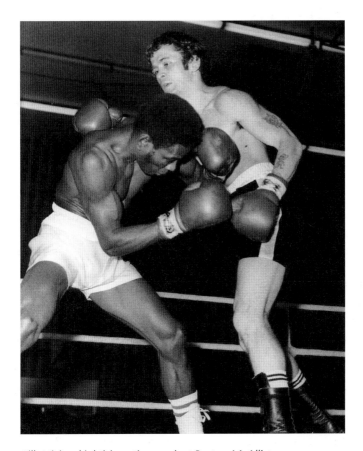

Billy Vivian (right) in action against Barton McAllister

Afan Lido on July 10, 1978, and after a tough 10 rounds in which fortunes swayed both ways, it was Billy's arm raised at the end.

A lack of potential challengers meant he was never to defend the throne, resuming his career-long role as the travelling instructor in learning fights for local favourites up and down the land. Now managed by Reading-based Bev Walker, Vivian was training himself in a converted garage at the Butchers' Arms in Pontsticill, then run by his father, while visiting gyms across South Wales to find sparring.

When Londoner Vernon Vanriel halted him in two rounds, Vivian realised that the old spark was no longer there and hung up the gloves. He spent a while as a trainer at Tre-Ifor ABC, but gave it up because of the travel involved in his work as a steel erector.

JOHNNY WALL
(1956–)

🥊 Welsh Lightweight Champion 1977–78

There was a special aura about the Welsh lightweight title for 20-odd years towards the end of the last century. And the man who did more than anyone to establish that tradition was the dustcart driver from Dowlais.

His belt-winning showdown with fellow-townsman Martyn Galleozzie set the standard in what many old-timers still insist is the best bout they have ever seen. If his defences against Billy Vivian, Dil Collins and eventual conqueror Kelvin Webber did not quite match those 10 rounds of mayhem, they were still pretty good, adding to the reputation of national wars at 9st 9lb that featured the likes of Andy Williams and Mervyn Bennett before Welsh championship activity sadly declined in recent years.

Hereford-born Wall – the family moved to Merthyr when he was six – became interested in boxing when his father took him to watch his friend,

Johnny Wall

Gerald Jones, sparring with Howard Winstone. Young Johnny was eight when he asked Eddie Thomas if he could join the gym, but the maestro pointed out he was a bit young and needed to serve his time in the amateurs first. So he began with the Courthouse club, upstairs at Merthyr Labour Club, learning the ropes from Danny Galeozzi, father of his future foe. A Welsh junior crown was followed by international vests at senior level.

He was still only 18 when he turned pro as a feather, the first managerial signing of former pro and new manager George Evans, who found him regular work in London. Not that he was fazed by travelling, marking his debut with a points win over previously unbeaten prospect Mark Bliss on the last-ever show at the historic Shoreditch Town Hall – and totally unaware of a bomb scare in the middle of the action.

Despite twice being held to draws by Midlander Billy Smart, Johnny remained undefeated in his first nine outings and was booked to top the bill in his first appearance at Rhydycar Leisure Centre, against 60-fight journeyman Barton McAllister. The Londoner arrived just 20 minutes before the start of Eddie Thomas's sell-out charity show, but was still alert enough to take an eight-round decision – and, rather embarrassingly, the shamefaced Wall had to return to the ring to receive an award for the Welsh Young Boxer of the Year.

There were further setbacks when former victim Johnny Claydon twice outscored the Merthyr man – Claydon stopped Jim Watt next time out, so he was no mug – and 1976 ended with a half-point loss to cross-town rival Galleozzie at the Rhondda Sports Centre in a thrilling appetiser for their title clash less than three months later.

Johnny as he looks today

Martyn had acquired the national belt in the interim, but local bragging rights were at least as significant when the pair came together at Rhydycar on February 15, 1977, and the ill-feeling was clear from the first bell. Perhaps without the mutual animosity, it would have been a lesser fight, as both men scorned defence and stood toe-to-toe for the duration.

Wall whips in a left hook in his war with Martyn Galleozzie

There were inevitable battle scars: both bled heavily from the nose, while Wall was cut between the eyes and under the chin, Galleozzie suffering a bad gash along the left eyebrow in the last. Johnny recovered from a slow start to take command, but a final-round left hook almost turned matters in Martyn's favour. Wall survived, however, to take a clear victory from world-class official Jim Brimmell, who described the contest as the greatest he had refereed in his entire globetrotting career.

The Cardiffian had just a half a point between Johnny and first challenger Billy Vivian at Ebbw Vale after another cracking scrap in which Wall's workrate overcame the Gurnos stylist's cleverer moves. Brimmell was again the third man when Johnny repelled Llantwit Major's Dil Collins on neutral ground at the National Sporting Club, although the real drama preceded the fight, when the car ferrying Wall, manager Evans and trainer Joe Beckett to London crashed on the M4. Incredibly, nobody was seriously hurt, but Johnny could barely raise his left arm above the shoulder and needed a pain-killing jab to see him through.

Wall's next defence proved a step too far, although Porth toolmaker Kelvin Webber had lost four in a row going into their encounter at the Afan Lido on March 20, 1978. The Rhondda boy ignored the formbook, however, and a below-par champion was clearly outpointed – but only after another all-action display, of course.

A stoppage loss to Mick Bell in Scotland the following month led Johnny to call it a day, although he made a brief and painful reappearance at light-welter in 1983 when hard-hitting John Andrews shattered dreams of a comeback inside two rounds.

FREDDIE WELSH
(1886–1927)

- **World Lightweight Champion 1914–17**

- **European Lightweight Champion 1909–11, 1912–14**

- **Empire Lightweight Champion 1912–14**

- **British Lightweight Champion 1909–11, 1912–19**

T
he man who took his nationality as a surname was, ironically, less like a Welsh fighter than most.

Where the majority of his contemporaries emerged from the depths of the pit to perform between the ropes, the products of a predominantly working-class society, Frederick Hall Thomas was the son of an auctioneer and a hotelier's daughter and attended a series of fee-paying schools.

In an era when a juicy steak – for those who could afford it – was the favoured route to a muscular fitness, the man from Pontypridd professed to be a vegetarian, training on milk, cereals, fruit and nuts.

And while many of his fellows read nothing more uplifting than the *Sporting Life*, Freddie was said to peruse the works of Epictetus and Ruskin while undergoing his daily massage. Not merely did he study the great writers, he inspired them: he was reputedly the template for Scott Fitzgerald's enigmatic hero, Jay Gatsby.

In addition – and it may explain some of the more outlandish claims hinted at above – he was the first British boxer to understand the benefit of publicity. Throughout his time in the States, he sent a steady stream of telegrams to journalists in his homeland, to make sure that, while he was out of sight, he would never be out of mind.

Freddie Welsh, student of physical culture

Elizabeth and John Thomas with their children, Kate, Stanley and young Freddie in the sailor suit

He posed enthusiastically for pictures in strange locations with exotic companions, with the result that he was recognised across all strata of American society and mingled readily with film stars and literary giants.

None of which would have made any difference if he hadn't been able to fight.

A career in the ring seemed improbable when the young Thomas first entered this world in a house in Morgan Street, close to the coal-black waters of the River Taff as it made its way through the centre of the fastest-growing town in Wales. When he was still a baby, his mother, Elizabeth, took over the nearby Bridge House Hotel and often paused between serving guests to count the ribs of her sickly first-born and wonder if he would make it into adulthood.

As the lad grew, his father had one obvious method for building up his delicate frame. Middle-class John Thomas may have become, but his father, Morgan, had been a noted mountain fighter and a love of fisticuffs was in the blood. He wrapped the hands of young Fred and his baby brother, Stanley, in towels and set them to sparring in the pub bar.

Unfortunately, John Thomas died and the children – there was also a girl, Kate – were dispersed among relatives. For Freddie there was also boarding school, where the need to deal with older bullies gave him every opportunity to indulge the love of fighting that had earned him respect on the streets of Ponty.

He eventually returned to the Bridge House and a new stepfather, taking up a position as an apprentice machinist. It proved too restrictive for an ambitious young man and he and two friends soon responded to newspaper adverts proclaiming the delights of a new life in Canada. Elizabeth was eventually persuaded to fund his journey and waved farewell to her 16-year-old offspring.

The streets of the New World were not paved with the expected gold. After a series of poorly paid jobs, Freddie began to feel homesick and worked his passage on a cattle boat to be back for Christmas. Life in Wales soon palled, however, and, despite his mother's qualms, he decided to cross the Atlantic again.

Once more, there was a less than generous welcome from local employers and the teenager took to travelling in search of work, riding the rods with the hobos, and picking up jobs on farms and in meat-packing yards, while adding a few dollars in hastily arranged scraps around the camp sites. It was only when he reached New York City, about a year after landing, that he found himself a steady position – and a wife.

Freddie was an avid reader of *Physical Culture*, a magazine published by Bernarr Macfadden, a controversial advocate of the importance of exercise and fitness – even, would you believe, for women! The young Welshman acquired a post as boxing and wrestling instructor and soon fell for one of the institute's pupils, Fanny Weston.

Macfadden's enterprise collapsed in scandal over revealing posters, and Fred, leaving his bride-to-be to continue her studies in the Big Apple, sought gainful employ in Philadelphia. It was only when he was introduced to the promoter of the city's Broadway Athletic Club that he considered a proper career in the ring. Fearful his mother might get to hear of his exploits, he insisted on taking a new name and opted for "Fred Cymry". Fanny, told what it meant, pointed out that locals would find "Welsh" much easier. And so it began.

This was the era of the 'No Decision' bouts in Philadelphia, but the newcomer soon earned the plaudits of the ringside newspapermen whose opinions decided the destination of wagers, with those who backed the "Englishman"

Freddie and Fanny, now officially revealed as his wife

FRED WELSH'S MASCOT IS NOW A PRIZED MEMENTO.
The World's Light-Weight Champion's Watch, bearing his Mother's Portrait on its face.

Freddie's special watch with a portrait of his mother

(as he was generally called, despite the substantial hint in his adopted name) usually leaving the hall with their wallets bulging.

Freddie had established himself as a significant player by the time he headed home to see his ailing mother. She proved to be better than he had anticipated and the prodigal opted to show off his new skills while in the old homeland. Former amateur star Harry Marks, now a noted manager, took him in hand and his influence obtained a fight at the select National Sporting Club in London's Covent Garden. His opponent, Seaman Arthur Hayes, was regarded as British champion at 9st 2lb, and many thought Welsh overmatched; he despatched the sailor in six rounds and picked up a nice few bob in successful bets at advantageous odds.

A points win over the useful Young Joseph underlined his ability, before he returned to Wales to display his wares in his native valley. In his first outing at Ponty's Park Gymnastic Club, Freddie beat three men in quick succession, in a total of less than six rounds.

The next year saw him remain unbeaten, claiming the British 9st 8lb title with a points decision over Londoner Dick Lee at the Welsh National Athletic Club in Merthyr – at that time, before the establishment in 1909 of the division limits that, by and large, remain today, championships were available at two-pound intervals, though the autocratic NSC would only recognise those won on their premises.

Successful in the ring, maybe, but Freddie was less so outside the ropes. Many of his townsfolk considered him arrogant, his adopted American ways – and accent – alienating conservative and traditionalist opinion. He also left nobody in doubt as to his motivation: "I box for money, *not* for pleasure."

Somewhat disillusioned by his reception, Welsh headed back to the States, although he had converted enough locals to his side to be presented with a portrait and given a lively choral send-off at the town's railway station. The days of slumming it aboard ship were long gone. Freddie travelled from Liverpool in luxury on the *Lusitania*, which had just regained the Blue Riband for the fastest Atlantic crossing. As well as travelling in higher class, the Welshman was soon mixing with the best in the ring.

He found that meant dealing with outside pressures as well as those inflicted by the opponent. Packey McFarland, a tough, hard-hitting product of the Chicago stockyards, claimed an unbeaten record when he met Welsh in Milwaukee; he also had the backing of some influential people. Referee Malachy Hogan, an otherwise respected official who seemed to have a blind spot where fighters from the 'Windy City' were concerned, ignored a blatant low blow from McFarland and then, after Packey had finished the 10 rounds battered and bleeding, still raised the American's hand.

The pair met again, in Los Angeles, on US Independence Day. Former heavyweight champion Jim Jeffries was the promoter and also patrolled the ring. Freddie dominated the first half of the scheduled 25 rounds, until news arrived that Battling Nelson had dethroned world lightweight king Joe Gans that evening in San Francisco. Perhaps that information – a new titleholder would want to cash in against easier opponents than Welsh – distracted him, for McFarland controlled the later stages and it was his turn to be outraged when the outcome was announced as a draw.

Packey's vociferous objections prompted Jeffries to give up the "thankless job" of refereeing, probably to Freddie's relief. "He would put his hands on our biceps and push us back," complained Welsh afterwards, "and I can tell you that Jeff's hands felt as though they weighed a ton apiece."

Nelson's surprise victory had made life more complicated. 'The Durable Dane' promised Welsh a shot if he could knock out Frank Carsey: Freddie duly did so, but no title fight was forthcoming. Instead the Battler defeated a fading Gans – the old hero was to die of tuberculosis less than two years later – in a rematch which paid so generously that the need for cash ceased to be all-important. He no longer had any interest in facing the man from Wales.

Featherweight champion Abe Attell was also in California and Welsh took advantage. He kept his jab in the New Yorker's face and took a clear-cut decision over the smaller man, later to receive similar treatment from Freddie's countryman, Jim Driscoll.

By now Welsh and Fanny were wed, though the press were unaware of the fact. As she now travelled with Freddie, taking care of his unique training diet, she was always referred to as his cook. The boxer's sister, Kate, was also part of his entourage, thus maintaining the appearance of propriety.

The desired showdown with Nelson was no nearer when a telegram reached Welsh from Britain offering him £1,000 for a British title challenge to the winner of Johnny Summers's forthcoming defence against Jimmy Britt. There was also talk of Lord Lonsdale presenting a bejewelled belt to each national champion. It was time to go home.

His constant barrage of letters and telegrams had borne fruit. Thousands welcomed him in Cardiff,

Always one for a photo-opportunity: Freddie meets an ostrich in California

Pontypridd – where no fewer than four brass bands took part in the procession – and Merthyr, where his mother now lived.

For his first appearance on home soil, a syndicate of Pontypridd businessmen put up a £550 purse for Welsh to meet old foe Young Joseph at Mountain Ash, where the Eisteddfod Pavilion was to be converted to hold 10,000 people. It may sound a paltry sum today, but in 1909 was four times more than for any previous bout in Wales.

The money men were more than pleased when a full house meant receipts of £4,000, while Freddie rewarded those in attendance with a display of fast-paced boxing that was totally different from the normal domestic fare, his wide repertoire of unorthodox punches including a blow to the kidneys which soon had the East Ender's back red raw. Joseph was a beaten man long before the low blows which brought him disqualification in the 11th round.

As Freddie and Fanny – their marriage still a secret as Welsh, like a latter-day pop star, sustained the dreams of his many female fans, who were allowed free entry to his training sessions – toured the museums and art galleries of the Low Countries, there came a challenge from representatives of one Henri Piet, a Frenchman, and the bout, with the European title at stake, was booked for Mountain Ash on August 23, 1909. Few pundits gave Piet much chance, while Welsh's own attitude might be discerned in the fact that he broke his drive from Cardiff to watch a "world championship" half-mile race in Ponty, only reaching the packed arena after the early bouts had begun. In fact, Henri showed a fair amount of skill, although he had taken a systematic beating by the time he raised his arms in surrender in the 12th, having injured a knee. He died a war hero six years later.

Despite the fulminations of local ministers lamenting such events as leading to damnation, Freddie returned to the Cynon Valley to knock out Londoner Joe Fletcher before finally facing Summers at the NSC on November 8, 1909.

Originally from Middlesbrough, though based at Canning Town, Summers had twice beaten Britt to confirm himself as the Welshman's only real rival at lightweight. But he was never going to lay serious claim to the first Lonsdale Belt ever to be contested. Blood poured from his nose from an early stage and there were no dissenters when Freddie was presented with his ornate prize.

Welsh enjoyed life as champion, appearing in music halls and relishing the late nights which followed. But his mind was brought back to boxing one day as he strolled down the Strand and was hailed by an American voice. Old foe McFarland was in town and had just learned that Ad Wolgast, who had appeared on their undercards, had beaten Nelson in what is recalled as one of the dirtiest title fights of all time. The two rivals realised that a third meeting between them would be the best way to advertise their suitability for a clash with the new monarch.

Many at the NSC disliked Welsh's demeanour – "I have never been able to bow down to rules and regulations," agreed Freddie – and saw Packey as the man to put him in his place. It produced a strange polarisation of opinion in the public prints: the British press, almost to a scribe, took McFarland's part, while their American counterparts backed Welsh.

When the talking was over, a record attendance packed the Covent Garden venue for a bout billed as for the world title, though both men knew that belonged to Wolgast. McFarland took early command and used his extra weight to bully Welsh, ripping uppercuts through the home fighter's guard. Even though Freddie came back in the closing stages, aristocratic eyebrows were raised in surprise when a draw was announced. Indeed, some public school voices were heard to utter threats to referee Tom Scott, who officiated at only one more show before being committed to a psychiatric hospital, where he spent his remaining years.

Welsh began to think of returning to the States, but there was a rising clamour for him to face a challenge from much closer to home. Jim Driscoll, who received a full measure of the love of both the public and the NSC which was denied Freddie, had long since fallen out with his one-time friend and sparring partner. Terms were agreed for the duo to settle matters at the American Skating Rink in Cardiff's Westgate Street, where the valley supporters nevertheless outnumbered the city slickers, despite the strikes that had paralysed the coalfield.

It was a classic confrontation between old-style British boxing from range and American in-fighting, in which the rougher, tougher transatlantic version came out on top. With NSC boss 'Peggy' Bettinson refereeing from ringside, Welsh was allowed to escape unpunished for a multitude of sins, with elbows, head and thumbs distributed liberally amid the legal blows. Even they included repeated attention to the damaged ear with which 'Peerless Jim' had entered the ring, plus his specialist kidney punches, both offending the sensibilities of those who backed Driscoll.

Eventually, the Cardiffian's suspect temper let him down. He forced Freddie back across the ring with a series of butts so blatant that even Bettinson could not miss them. The august figure rose from his chair and immediately disqualified Jim. As Driscoll wept, bedlam broke out as the two seconds, followed by hundreds of partisans on both sides, sought to make their points as forcefully as possible.

Despite calls for a rematch, wiser counsels prevailed and the pair went their separate ways. For Welsh it meant finally defending the Lonsdale Belt he had won 15 months earlier. The NSC at last had someone they regarded as a suitable challenger: Londoner Matt Wells, a four-time ABA champion and former Olympian, whose pro career was just four days longer than Freddie's reign as champion.

The critics labelled their clash, on February 27, 1911, a mismatch. But Wells had a secret weapon, a trainer named Dai Dollings. The Swansea man, regarded as the Freddie Roach of his day, had studied Welsh and noted his tendency to start slowly. He encouraged his charge to go all-out from the first bell of an encounter which the Pontypridd fighter took so lightly that he was prepared to overlook that fact that Matt was half a pound overweight, something that should really have ruled out title status.

With the club's members and guests overwhelmingly supporting Wells, the challenger followed Dollings's instructions to the letter. And even though Freddie came on strongly in the later rounds, it was not enough to save the day. At the end the referee pointed to the Londoner and wild cheers welcomed a new hero.

Wells, a renowned bleeder, was in such a mess as he passed through the club's kitchens to reach the dressing-rooms that the cook screamed and hid her face in an apron. When informed that this was the winner, she swore she did not want to see the loser. Yet Freddie was virtually unmarked, lamenting his carelessness – and the genius of a Welsh trainer.

Despite his defeat, the Americans were still keen to have Freddie back. An easy win over Pal Moore – who had beaten an ailing Driscoll – confirmed he had not regressed, something underlined on the West Coast by victory over tough Matty Baldwin. It earned Welsh what he had long been chasing, a shot in Los Angeles at world champion Wolgast. But on the eve of the bout Ad was struck down by appendicitis and the fight was off. An urgent search for a replacement foe came up with a young Californian named Willie Ritchie, who put up a decent show for a late substitute, but was clearly outpointed. He will figure again in this story.

Freddie toured the US and Canada before returning to London in a bid to retrieve his British and European honours from Wells. On November 11, 1912, he succeeded, dominating proceedings after his customary sluggish opening. All was again right in his world. Five weeks later, Welsh added the Empire title by outscoring Hughie Mehegan, an Antipodean visitor who had earlier beaten Wells, helped by a little pre-fight subterfuge. It was widely known that Freddie had suffered a cut eyebrow in sparring which had barely healed; to confuse Mehegan he wore a plaster into the ring – over the wrong eye!

As 1913 began, there was sadness outside the ring with the death of his mother. Inside it Freddie saw off two French challengers for his continental crown, halting both Paul Brevières, at Aberdare's Market Hall, and Raymond Vittet, in Sheffield, one of three scheduled 20-rounders Welsh fitted into seven days before setting sail for the States once more. While he had been away, Wolgast had lost his world championship on a disqualification, but only after being floored twice. The new holder? That man Ritchie.

From the moment he disembarked from the *Mauritania* in New York, Freddie was seeking out the new champion. But Willie was not an easy quarry, preferring to cash in on his new prominence with exhibitions and theatrical appearances. Welsh had to go down a similar route, boxing a series of local hopefuls, frequently in 'No Decision' bouts, interrupting his journey to reveal that he and his "cook", Fanny, had actually been married for the past eight years.

Negotiations for a meeting with Ritchie came up with a succession of dates and venues, but the showdown did not materialise until July 7, 1914, when the pair touched gloves at London's Olympia Theatre. It had proved hard bargaining. Impresario C.B. Cochran offered a $25,000 purse, but the American wanted double. Eventually, agreement was reached, the principals signed articles in New York and promptly headed for Britain, Welsh landing at Southampton, Ritchie, ironically, in Wales, at Fishguard. Final talks saw Willie happily opt for a British referee, Eugene Corri, and accept the British 9st 9lb weight limit, two pounds above that used in the US. To add to Freddie's contentment, Fanny gave birth to a daughter, Elizabeth, before leaving New York to join him.

At last the big one – Welsh signs for his world title chance with promoter C.B. Cochran between him and champion Willie Ritchie

A souvenir of the big occasion

The fight was publicised like no previous such event and the great and the good attended in numbers matched by those who had packed dozens of trains from Wales. The crowds outside were so thick that Welsh himself was unable to penetrate them and, at the time scheduled for the first bell, he had yet to reach the hall. Fortunately, he had already changed and when he finally made it, went straight from his car to the ring. Despite the lack of time to warm up, Freddie showed unaccustomed early aggression and enjoyed enough success for him to smile broadly as he returned to his corner after the opening session.

Ritchie's clubbing right hooks occasionally punished Welsh's moments of complacency, notably in the 13th, but the champion was becoming desperate, his wildness even resulting in one swing landing on the unfortunate Mr Corri. Fanny and her sister, who reached the venue even later than Freddie, were confident enough to move into ringside seats for the closing exchanges. Even before the official verdict, the Welsh fans were singing the anthem and their celebrations continued in the streets. Their hero was already back in the hotel to meet his little girl for the first time.

Heavily out of pocket as a result of the deal needed to persuade Ritchie to travel, Freddie, as Britain's first world lightweight king since Dick Burge in the 1890s, was looking to capitalise with a series of bouts on home soil and music hall appearances across Europe. But his "lap of honour" was barely underway when war broke out and there was neither time nor inclination for such fripperies. Boxers across the country signed up for a much bigger fight. Welsh, however, wife and baby in tow, was on board the *Olympic*, heading for New York.

There was criticism of his departure on both sides of the Atlantic, but nothing to get in the way of business. After a stint on the boards, Freddie began a campaign which involved seven contests in as many weeks – more than Ritchie had in his two-and-a-half-year reign – with a few decent men among his opponents, including former king Wolgast, who suffered his first stoppage loss when he retired with a damaged arm.

Although Freddie's title was technically at stake in many of his outings, it only applied if he was beaten inside the distance, and the selection of mainly inoffensive foes made sure there was little risk of that. More importantly to Welsh, for whom boxing was always a business rather than a vocation, he was pulling in much larger crowds than had paid to watch him before he could add the tag 'champion' alongside his name.

Welsh on the attack against a wary Ritchie

His circle of friends was also expanding, with the inclusion of politicians and playwrights, a feature that prompted the contempt of journalists who condemned him as one "who feels himself to be superior to his job".

The 'No Decision' legislation left power in the hands of the hacks, prompting numerous newspaper verdicts against him. Taking on contenders in their back yards boosted the gate, but gave local reporters the chance to laud their fellow-townsmen irrespective of what actually happened in the ring. In New York such votes were driven more by personal animosity. Freddie didn't care. He just counted the money.

The champion's readiness to challenge tradition was further shown when he persuaded the authorities at Madison Square Garden to ban smoking when he fought. Perhaps a few withdrawal symptoms contributed to the columnists' insistence that Welsh had lost a rematch with Ritchie there.

The exceptional defensive skills of the Pontypridd man, coupled with his innate caution, had the boxing establishment more and more irritated. No challenger came close to achieving the knockout needed to capture the title and there were increased demands for Welsh to risk his position in a jurisdiction that allowed proper decisions.

Freddie had no argument with the idea. Already thinking of retirement, he wanted to maximise his remaining earnings and manager Harry Pollok organised a newspaper poll to come up with the most deserving challenger. It opted for Chicago's Charley White, but it was more than a year before he had his chance. Meanwhile, another young man was building a following, a Jewish New Yorker called Benjamin Leiner, who boxed as Benny Leonard.

Leonard thrilled his supporters by giving Welsh a rough time in a 10-round meeting at the Garden, but their voices were silenced when Freddie, defying those who thought him in decline, handed out a lesson in a rematch at Brooklyn's Washington Park Athletic Club. Two months later, more than two years after ascending the throne, the champion finally faced a legitimate contender in a 20-round bout under title conditions, taking on the patient White in Colorado Springs.

Freddie was happy to do so, not merely for the hefty purse involved, but because he was confident he would retain what he called "the lightweight bonnet", insisting that there was "no use going to the haberdasher for another when this one fits so well". Nevertheless, he came close to losing both bonnet and belt, although the fight almost never happened.

A planned railway strike was averted only just in time to enable fans to travel and, once they were in the arena, one of the stands collapsed, sending around 400 occupants plummeting to the ground. One man was killed, while another 150 people were badly injured. To help the emergency services deal with the casualties, more than 2,000 latecomers were turned away. But the bout went ahead.

Freddie proceeded to box on the retreat, skilfully forcing White to face the blistering summer sun. His trombone left bloodied Charley's face and, despite the American's aggression, saw him through to victory in the opinion of referee Billy Roche and most ringsiders. Others, however, reacted to the decision with a hail of cushions and other missiles and the third man had to be rushed through the angry crowd to a getaway car.

Welsh went back to the circuit of 'No Decision' bouts, where local pressmen frequently awarded the palm to their "homeboys", although everyone agreed that Freddie had beaten the biggest name among his opponents, former ruler Nelson. The Battler, close to 35, never boxed again.

In the spring of 1917 the US joined the war and Freddie was among the first to enlist, confirming that America was now his permanent home. His campaign in the ring, however, was in decline. Suddenly, newspaper decisions against him were less easily put down to biased pressmen. Within a week he lost three such verdicts, the last to featherweight king Johnny Kilbane. It was no way to prepare for another meeting with the rapidly improving Leonard, at the Manhattan Sporting Club on May 28, 1917.

Freddie Welsh, the inspiration for Jay Gatsby?

Freddie was as confident as ever. When the referee explained the rules pre-fight, he replied, "Do you mean I've got to go to a neutral corner *every* time I knock him down?"

Once again, being in New York, it was a 'No Decision' contest and Welsh firmly believed that nobody could manage the stoppage win required to lift the championship. This time he was wrong. Leonard abandoned previously futile assaults on his ever-moving head and focussed on the body. The plan succeeded, gradually drawing Freddie's hands down to protect his increasingly sore midriff. At last, the opening was there and seconds after the bell rang to signal the ninth of 10 allotted rounds, a big right crashed into Welsh's temple and staggered him.

Benny, a full decade younger, kept banging away. Exhausted, Freddie was floored, but, unwisely, rose immediately. Another barrage sent him back to the canvas. After a third knockdown, he had to use the ropes to clamber back up, but his left arm became caught and he could not defend himself as Leonard went for the kill. Referee Billy McPartland stopped the action to free him, but Welsh staggered across the ring and collapsed over the middle rope. His reign was over. And just to make things worse, manager Pollok had bet the whole purse on his man to win.

Welsh, while conceding the New Yorker's superiority, desperately maintained that he was still the champion as he had not been counted out. The complaint was made without conviction – and certainly without hope of success. It was time to follow a long-held dream of running a health farm on the 160-acre property he had already bought at Long Hill, New Jersey.

But after a few months Welsh was missing the bright lights. There were also military duties at a Washington hospital, where he worked with wounded soldiers. Within a year the farm was up for sale, but even at a knockdown $20,000 – a third of what he had paid for it when it was run-down and ramshackle – there were no takers. And there was more trouble on the way, featuring estranged manager Pollok.

The pair unexpectedly found themselves at the same restaurant. A violent argument ended with Welsh pushing his meal to one side to indulge in a little Tyson-esque dining on Pollok's right ear. Harry was rushed to hospital with the detached lobe in an ice-bucket; Freddie was carted off to the cells. Only Pollok's failure to press charges saved the former champion from a jail term.

Harry moved to California as a promoter, but in 1933 shot himself at his luxurious home. By then, his former fighter had been dead for six years.

There was little business at the health farm and keen gambler Welsh was losing regularly on the horses. Meanwhile boxing in the 'Big Apple' had taken on a new lease of life with the passing of the Walker Law, which legalised the

World Champion Lightweight
Boxer (1914-17) trained here

FREDDIE WELSH
(Frederick Hall Thomas)

1886 - 1927

Bu Pencampwr Bocsio Pwysau
Ysgafn y Byd (1914-17)
yn hyfforddi yma

Pontypridd remembers Freddie with a plaque on the old Clarence Hotel, where he once trained

sport in the state. That, allied to increasing money worries, inevitably pushed him towards a comeback.

He saw off four no-hopers and began talking of a rematch with Leonard. But he could only draw with Canadian Clonie Tait in Winnipeg and then, having persuaded a New York club to give him an opportunity, lost a wide decision to the ordinary Archie Walker. Even Freddie knew the game was up.

A trip home revealed that, at 37, he no longer held any interest for British fight folk. He refereed a few bouts in Wales, but departed for the States after just two months. The farm had a period of comparative prosperity, thanks partly to the patronage of Jack Dempsey, but it did not last. By the mid-1920s Welsh's own health was deteriorating, not helped by a serious fondness for the drink.

The farm had to be sold to meet increasing debts and he moved into cheap lodgings, while Fanny left to take the post of housekeeper in a rather more sophisticated establishment, the St Paul Hotel, where they had once rented a suite. The formerly unhittable champion was beaten up in a small-hours street brawl, only a generous magistrate saving him from prison. Just over a week later, Freddie Welsh was found dead on the floor of his room.

CHRIS WILLIAMS
(1977–)

🥊 Welsh Super-Featherweight Champion   1999–2000

Boxing was always likely to attract the youngster from the Gurnos estate. After all, father Howard fought as a pro in the 1980s, while grandfather Tommy was an Army champion and a great-grandfather had a few bouts as an amateur.

Chris began to follow their footsteps as a 10-year-old with Merthyr ABC, but when trainer Gareth Donovan left the club, the boy joined him in exile at the Highfields set-up in Cardiff before his mentor established Merthyr Ex-Servicemen's ABC in 1996. His wanderings did not prevent an outstanding junior career.

A clutch of Welsh titles – and three victories over England in schoolboy internationals – were supplemented by two British Schools triumphs and a pair of Gaelic Games gold medals. His first season as a senior was marked by a Welsh ABA flyweight title in 1995, though he did not defend it the following year.

A pro career was inevitable. With Donovan still looking after his training and Dai Gardiner as manager, the future looked bright. Then came his debut at a chilly National Ice Rink – and disaster. Just 56 seconds into his all-southpaw meeting with fellow first-timer John Matthews, referee Mike Heatherwick was diving in to rescue the Merthyr teenager.

There were to be three defeats in Williams's first four outings. Yet the solitary victory came on points over future British and WBU ruler Michael Gomez before his own Manchester fans. It was an indication that the talent was there.

A run of four straight wins seemed to have set Chris's career on an even keel, but an injured

Chris Williams (left) with Miguel Matthews

ankle brought a premature end to a wild and woolly encounter with Ugandan Isaac Sebaduuka and began a sequence of five bouts without success, although he did deck unbeaten Scouser Tony Mulholland en route to a draw. There was no disgrace in losing a decision to former WBO champion Barry Jones, in the Cardiffian's first action following a brain-scan scare, while a swollen-shut eye brought early defeat against former Olympian David Burke.

Next up, however, came the highlight of Williams's pro career – and it came before his own people at Rhydycar Sports Centre on September 14, 1999. At stake was the vacant Welsh super-feather title; in the opposite corner Miguel Matthews, a Swansea Valley coalman in his 107th paid fight. The veteran contributed in full to 10 thrilling rounds, although a tendency to come in with his head low saw Chris repeatedly gesturing in dismay and eventually prompted referee Roddy Evans to dock the Ystalyfera man a point in the seventh. It more or less confirmed the outcome, with the local boy receiving a 97–94 scoreline.

A return to Rhydycar saw Williams beat Swansea's Marc Smith, before dropping a points verdict to future British champion Roy Rutherford despite flooring the Midlander twice. There was revenge over previous conqueror Craig Spacie, but a defeat by transplanted Mongolian Choi Tseveenpurev, later to wear a WBU belt, prompted Chris to call it a day.

A former postman, he now works for British Rail and lives in Penydarren with his girlfriend and two daughters.

HOWARD WINSTONE
(1939–2000)

World Featherweight Champion   1968

European Featherweight Champion   1963–67

British Featherweight Champion   1961–69

Howard Winstone was a curly-headed kid selling newspapers when he first met Eddie Thomas. Eddie was champion of Britain, Europe and the Empire, and a local idol: no child of Merthyr had achieved such greatness since Joseph Parry wrote *Myfanwy*. He took a paper, gave the boy two bob, told him to keep the change, and thought no more of it. The 12-year-old Howard, on the other hand, could talk of nothing else for days.

He was already hooked on boxing. As a scruffy youngster in the streets of Penydarren, he would run a mile rather than fight, so his father – also Howard – gave him a pair of gloves and hung a punchbag on a tree in the garden. Sparring sessions in the kitchen led to tuition from Ephraim Hamer, the man who had trained his hero Thomas, and then former fighter Billy Evans.

He had already won a string of schools titles when a new gym opened near his home, run by the man who had bought that paper five years earlier. Howard joined him there, and Eddie Thomas was in the corner in 1958, when an ABA bantamweight title was a mere prelude to that unforgettable night in Cardiff's Sophia Gardens Pavilion, the Merthyr boy standing on a dais, tears in his eyes and an Empire Games gold medal around his neck, as his ecstatic countrymen sang *Hen Wlad Fy Nhadau*.

It was an amazing feat for someone who had lost the tips of three fingers on his right hand in an accident two years earlier at the toy factory where he worked. When the toymakers sacked him for taking time off to box, there was only one way

Howard Winstone

Winstone wins the only gold medal for the Empire Games hosts

to look after his young wife and two sons – by turning pro. The inevitable choice as manager: Eddie Thomas.

There were no easy touches for the tyro, but he still managed to build a record of 24 wins in as many months. There were a few fellow-countrymen among his victims: Welsh feather king Terry Rees, London-born, but qualified through parents from the Rhondda, Cardiffian Gordon Blakey, floored twice, but eventually beaten by a swollen and cut right eye, and another son of the capital, Phil Jones, who had lost only once previously in 22 bouts.

Australian Olympian Noel Hazard, former European challenger Sergio Milan and Belgian champion Jean Renard were also seen off, but Howard's progress was best illustrated by his victories over two Africans: Nigerian Roy Jacobs, who had drawn with British titleholder Terry Spinks, and outstanding Ghanaian Floyd Robertson, whose Empire crown was not at stake, were each outscored over 10 rounds.

A challenge to baby-faced Cockney Spinks was inevitable and lucrative, the pair earning a record £12,055 purse. The 23-year-old former stable lad from Canning Town had won Olympic flyweight gold in Melbourne five years earlier, and the punters at Wembley on May 2, 1961, were handed programmes in that colour to mark "The Clash of the Golden Boys".

The meal matched the menu. It was a banquet of brilliant boxing, with master chef Winstone cooking up a series of variations on that staple ingredient, the straight left. His accuracy of punch was phenomenal, with Spinks's occasional counters and brave flurries merely diversions on Howard's road to the championship.

"He was a very fast boy, Spinks," recalled Howard. "But so was I. And I caught up with him eventually."

A young Howard on the bag with Danny Reardon

He did, indeed. The champion began to disintegrate. At the end of the 10th, there was nothing left. Terry remained on his stool, and Wales had her first featherweight champion since World War I. Only after the belt had been placed around his waist did Howard reveal that his left hand had gone in the second round!

There were a couple of successful defences – the first saw Glasgow-based Ulsterman Derry Treanor halted in the 14th round and forced into retirement, the other featured crewcut Cardiff steelworker Harry Carroll, beaten in six rounds on his home ground at Maindy Stadium to earn Winstone a Lonsdale Belt to keep – before disaster struck. An unsung lightweight from Michigan, one Leroy 'Honeyboy' Jeffery, floored Howard three times and stopped him in two rounds. Watching was the great Sugar Ray Robinson, who told Howard: "I had 40 fights before I was beaten, but I learned more from that defeat than from all the wins."

Determined to prove that he, too, would learn, Winstone travelled to Scotland to repel a challenge from Johnny Morrissey, a curly-headed plumber from Lanarkshire, watched by hundreds of Welsh rugby fans en route to Murrayfield two days later.

He then added the European crown with a 14th-round stoppage of Italian Alberto Serti, at Maindy Stadium on July 9, 1963. Howard had already stopped Gracieux Lamperti, the Frenchman Serti had dethroned, and was hot favourite to do the same to the Italian. In the end, it took him 14 rounds, although French referee Georges Gondre could easily have stepped in sooner as Winstone dominated with a superb display of left-hand work, backed up by a tight defence. He picked up a nick near the left eye late on, but merely stepped up the pace, although the brave visitor was still on his feet when the third man finally intervened.

First up to challenge the new double champion was a familiar face: Billy Calvert, from Sheffield, twice beaten by Howard on his way up, had shocked the pundits by knocking out fancied Scot Bobby Fisher in a final eliminator. And when he met Winstone for the belts at Coney Beach, he gave him more trouble than anyone had expected. The man they called 'Cowboy' had beaten Jeffery just three weeks after the American had upset Howard and he took that self-belief into the ring against his former conqueror. He smothered the Welshman's work and scored well to the body in a non-stop struggle, which left the champion relieved to have his arm raised after going 15 rounds for the first time.

Winstone, bronzed from a holiday in Majorca, earned a second Lonsdale Belt to keep with a more comfortable points success over Glaswegian John O'Brien, in a fight controversially staged at the exclusive National Sporting Club's Café Royal headquarters in the West End. At first, the Board of

Winstone with Merthyr promoter Bill Long

Control would not recognise it as a British title defence because the public could not attend, an ironic reversal of the situation half a century earlier when national champions could only be crowned within the portals of the NSC. Eventually, the Board relented, originally for that one fight only, though many more were to follow.

Howard was back in the public gaze a month later, but fans at Olympia saw referee Jack Hart rule that he had lost to Californian Don Johnson. Hart was due to handle Winstone's next outing, too, but Eddie's protests had him replaced by Harry Gibbs when the Merthyr Marvel met Nigerian Joe Rafiu King at Wembley. King, who claimed to have been indulging in pre-fight prophecy before new world heavyweight ruler Muhammad Ali, forecast a win in four sessions: "One for the Queen's new baby, one for the promoter, one for the public and one for me!"

He nearly achieved his goal in just two, flooring Winstone, and only a strange reluctance to follow up in the third – perhaps he was waiting for his predicted fourth – allowed Howard to recover and edge a verdict that was far too close for comfort.

Turning his attention to the Continent, Winstone beat off challenges from Italian champion Lino Mastellaro, in eight, and his French counterpart, Yves Desmarets, on points, the latter contest taking place in Rome after a row between the Board and the European Boxing Union meant home promoters were unable to bid. However, it needed revenge over Johnson at Carmarthen before the WBC nominated Winstone as the next challenger to the world champion, a Mexican lorry driver's son called Vicente Samuel Saldívar García. The Welshman completed his preparation at Blackpool with a hard 10-round victory over a Madrid-based Cuban, José Legrá. The name will reappear in this story.

A substantial cheque from Harry Levene persuaded Saldívar to defend at London's Earls Court on September 7, 1965. One of nine children raised in a Mexico City slum, the former printer's apprentice now had his own business, but this material security had not led to any lessening of ambition, as Winstone was to discover – in triplicate.

The Welshman trained by chopping down trees with a 14lb axe blunted to make the task harder. It was no easier to hack down Saldívar. The Mexican's southpaw stance, chin tucked in behind his right shoulder, denied Howard the target usually offered his pea-shooter left, and he was forced to discard his customary elegance in favour of hooks and greater use of the right hand. Vicente's only loss in 29 bouts had been on disqualification, and the rough edges showed, but the legal assaults were sufficient to build up a solid lead by the halfway mark. Howard had his share of success, leaving the visitor's face red and bruised, but he was showing signs of weariness, while the 22-year-old Mexican's stamina seemed inexhaust-

Howard, Eddie Thomas and promoter Harry Levene sign contracts for the second Saldívar fight

ible. The 14th had Winstone trapped in a corner, then floundering across the ring before the relentless fists of the confident champion. But Saldívar was unable to finish it, and Howard's last-round rally gave his supporters hope, only for London referee Bill Williams to turn to the Mexican at the end.

The Merthyr man was convinced he had won, and brushed off Eddie's suggestion that he should call it a day. Business was brisk in Europe, with Andrea Silanos halted in the last in Sardinia and Belgian Jean de Keers stopped on cuts in London, while Johnson was beaten in a rubber match, controversially disqualified for low blows that only referee Jack Lord seemed to notice. There was also an all-Welsh title clash at Aberavon with Lennie 'The Lion' Williams, a 22-year-old colliery blacksmith from Maesteg, who was tamed in eight rounds.

Howard was ready for another try at Saldívar, at Ninian Park, Cardiff, on June 15, 1967. Asked if he was worried about travelling to Winstone's back yard, manager Adolfo Pérez replied, "No, señor – wherever he is, a good rooster can crow." Most of the rather disappointing crowd believed Saldívar had been knocked off his perch after one of the best fights ever seen in Wales; alas for Howard, one of those who disagreed was referee Wally Thom.

This time Winstone stuck to what he did best. He boxed. And he boxed with such consummate skill that it took the Mexican some time to find an answer. The solution he came up with proved decisive: two-fisted attacks to the body that chipped away at the Welshman's strength. But their effect was

Howard and his ever-present mentor, Eddie Thomas

gradual, and the early rounds saw Howard making Saldívar miss with sidesteps that would have raised a chorus of "Olé" in a Mexican bull-ring. Two planeloads of sombrero-waving supporters had flown in to cheer the champion, but they had little opportunity as Winstone's accurate punches picked their man off repeatedly, and there were worried expressions in the holder's corner.

Howard, however, was looking marked by the ninth, and the constant body shots began to take their toll. It became harder to stay out of trouble, and then, in the 14th, impossible. A two-fisted salvo sent Winstone down for eight; when he rose, he sagged defenceless on the ropes as the Mexican poured in right hands, manager Thomas resisting the temptation to surrender only in the belief that if his charge could somehow stay upright the title was his. The longed-for bell eventually brought relief, Eddie spraying him with champagne in a desperate bid to revive that earlier spark. To an extent, it worked. Driven on by his boundless courage, Winstone somehow managed to fend off the champion's punches through that endless last round. And then came a blow harder to take than any thrown by Saldívar: Mr Thom walked to the Mexican's corner and lifted his arm.

Howard refused to believe that the champion was the better man, and insisted Eddie get him another shot. Saldívar agreed, but it had to be in Mexico City, with its 7,000-foot altitude, which prompted the Welsh team to fly out three weeks early. The challenger's arrival was not auspicious, his plane being struck by lightning as they came in to land. Not that Howard was worried: he slept like a baby until they were safely on the ground. Eddie was less fortunate. Having already angered the Mexican media by implying that Saldívar had used stimulants in Cardiff, he was confined to bed with a touch of pneumonia.

It's all over for Winstone as the towel comes in to end the third Saldívar scrap in Mexico City

The promoters had organised a training camp at Ixtapán de la Sal, high in the mountains, where Howard could spar with travelling companion Billy Thomas, but days of torrential rain prompted Eddie to return to Mexico City. Their first two attempts were blocked by landslides, but the group finally made it and resumed their preparation at an indoor skating rink.

Despite the disruption, Winstone was confident. "I made a couple of mistakes the first time and one mistake the second," he said. "This time there'll be no mistakes."

The Merthyr man was given a tremendous ovation from the fans when he climbed through the ropes at the brand-new Aztec Stadium on October 14, 1967. Saldívar's welcome was less friendly: a right hook which made the Welshman's knees buckle. Nevertheless, the pattern of the second fight was repeated, with Howard picking up points with that effortless left, while the champion worked downstairs. The outcome, too, was similar. Winstone's massive lead counted for nothing as Vicente wore him down, and the rarefied atmosphere took its toll.

"Suddenly, in the ninth, it was like my legs had been chopped from under me," Howard remembered. "I couldn't breathe properly and I couldn't move like I wanted to."

The end came in the 12th. The Welshman took a pounding on the ropes before subsiding to the floor, blood streaming from his nose. He clambered up to face a murderous onslaught and was reeling round the ring when Eddie hurled in the towel and dragged his beaten warrior to sanctuary.

There was a sensation still to come. Saldívar announced his retirement from the ring – "I decided halfway through the fight" – and told the battered Winstone that he could still be No 1. The WBC agreed, matching him with Mitsunori Seki, a 26-year-old Japanese southpaw who had already failed in four attempts at a world title, two of them against Saldívar. Vicente was at the Albert Hall ringside to see his two victims battle it out on January 23, 1968.

Howard started sluggishly, with Seki ahead at the midway point. Both boxers had picked up cuts, with the Merthyr man's apparently the more serious, but he gradually took command, and an eighth-round assault had the fans chanting his name. One round later they were acclaiming a new champion. The pair came together awkwardly and as they parted a smear of blood appeared above Seki's right eye; as Winstone followed up, referee Roland Dakin stepped between them, peered at the Japanese and led him to his corner. Only when he walked across to grasp Howard's arm did the stunned watchers – inside and outside the ring – realise he had stopped the contest. Seki's camp were furious, but American promoter George Parnassus spoke for most others present: "Those Japs should be glad they've got an excuse to take home. Their boy would have been taken apart in the next couple of rounds."

The arguments were academic. For Winstone, the mountain had been climbed. Let the rest praise or protest; he was world champion.

There was to be little time for self-satisfaction. The following morning reality intruded, with a divorce court ringing the final bell on his stormy marriage to Benita. And, although he was named Welsh Sportsman of the Year for a third time, there was little left for him in the ring, either.

British junior lightweight champion Jimmy Anderson floored him in a catchweight bout, only wildness allowing Winstone to recover for a points win. The writing was on the wall. Nemesis would arrive in a familiar form: José Legrá, now a Spanish citizen who had assumed the mantle of European champion, stripped from the Welshman while he concentrated on higher things.

Legrá had lost only once – to Winstone that night at Blackpool three years earlier – since moving to Madrid from

Referee Roland Dakin examines the cut over Mitsunori Seki's eye – seconds later Winstone was a world champion

Castro's Cuba, where professional boxing was banned. Like Saldívar, José had risen from the depths of poverty. One of eight children, he was 15 when he was given a pair of boxing boots; they were the first shoes he had ever worn. Five years later, former pro Kid Tunero, himself a Cuban exile, heard of the youngster's promise and invited him to Spain. Only Howard now stood between Legrá and the fulfilment of both their dreams.

Retired champion Vicente Saldívar congratulates his successor

Only Howard! Such a dismissive statement would have been sacrilegious a few years earlier, but the cards were now dealt differently, with few aces in the Welshman's hand. Legrá was three inches taller, although Winstone had the longer reach. The Cuban-Spaniard was 25, a man in his prime; Howard was 29, with too many hard fights behind him. If the three wars with Saldívar had left the victor seeking retirement, how much more must they have taken out of the loser? It was no surprise that the bookmakers had José a clear pre-fight favourite, even though the pair were to meet, on July 24, 1968, before 11,000 Welshmen at Coney Beach, Porthcawl.

Yet the outcome was decided by none of these factors, rather by that unpredictable quirk of fate, an eye injury. And not merely a cut: with Eddie Thomas in the corner, a simple gash would have been a containable problem. The disaster that befell Winstone was something not even that genius of the swabstick could combat,

Old foe José Legrá is the first to challenge for Winstone's crown

and it happened before the bout was a minute old. The southpaw Legrá threw an unorthodox, round-arm right which caught the Welshman high on the face and sent him stumbling to the canvas. The singing fans were silenced as if a radio had been switched off. And even those at the back could see, as Howard rose to his feet, that his left eye was completely closed.

The challenger moved in. Winstone was briefly down again, but somehow, from beyond his despair he found the determination to battle on. Even after the end-of-round confirmation that there was no way of raising the purple curtain that hung between him and Legrá's right hand – he still hauled himself from his stool and went to meet his fate.

"The eye was closed tight," said Howard. "Eddie couldn't cut it because it was swollen from the top down. There was nothing we could do."

The European titleholder was a man of no little ability. He unveiled a variety of punches as he strove to finish off the wounded champion; Howard was able to defend against many, but not the right. What he could not see, he could not parry, nor evade. The patient Legrá chipped away, confident in the inevitability of his victory. Referee Harry Gibbs visited the Welsh corner in each interval, each time deciding with some reluctance that Winstone should

Howard Winstone is doubly honoured by his people, finding immortality as a statue and a Grogg

be allowed to continue. The brave man from Merthyr clung on to his crown until the fifth round, when Legrá staggered him with a succession of blows to the head, and Mr Gibbs finally ended the torture.

"I'd have beaten him if it wasn't for the eye," insisted Howard. "He never hurt me, but I couldn't see him coming. It felt terrible to lose that way."

It was 10 years to the day since Winstone had won his Empire Games gold. The journey was over. He would fight no more.

But there was still to be pain, from a troublesome back and legs that never forgave him for the years of strain. There were financial difficulties, for Howard, like so many, found that a boxing brain did not always imply a head for business. But there was happiness, too, with second wife Bronwen and a family in which the grandchildren reached double figures. He was awarded the M.B.E., like his mentor, Eddie Thomas, and became a Freeman of the Borough.

It reflected the enduring love of the people of Merthyr, demonstrated in the overflowing church where they bade him a final farewell in October 2000 and in the generosity which enabled the erection of a statue, forever a memorial to a fighting town's own world champion.

THE SUPPORTING CAST

However many boxers were selected for profiles in this book, there would be hundreds more with stories that deserved the telling. Let us give a nod to a handful, at least, in these closing pages.

How about Sammy Jennings, from Dowlais, who claimed the title of 'Boy Champion of the World' after beating Young Joey Smith on New Year's Day, 1907, while weighing just 4st 7lb? The fight came after Cardiff RFC had defeated the Springboks and was watched by both teams.

Another "midget", as they called them in those days, was Young Freddie Welsh. The son of Pontypridd manager Wyndham Williams, he was just seven when he had his first bout and a loss in Liverpool in his late teens was said to have been his first in 142 contests, even if most of those had ended in diplomatic draws.

Boxing at Merthyr Labour Club around 1931

Young Freddie later fought successfully in Australia, something matched by Merthyr Vale's Jack Jones, a lightweight title claimant who became a bit of a star Down Under in the 1920s.

The first man to earn a widespread reputation was another Jack Jones, a farm boy from Penderyn, alias Shoni Sgubor Fawr, renowned as the 'Emperor of China' for his domination of that notorious slum near the river. Shoni fought the champion of the Cyfarthfa Works, John Nash, in a special bout to celebrate the completion of the Taff Vale Railway in 1841. He later moved to Pontyberem, became a hired thug for the Daughters of Rebecca and was transported to Tasmania.

Then there was William Lee, a mountain fighter from Pontypridd, known as 'Mother' Lee, after his own Mam, a well-known gipsy. When a famous evangelist, Tennyson Smith, visited the town to persuade the inhabitants of the virtues of being teetotal – no easy task in Ponty, then or now – he took a nine-gallon cask of ale to the Berw Bridge, intending to pour it into the river. The

Young Freddie Welsh

barrel slipped into the water before Smith could open it and 'Mother' promptly dived to the rescue. He and his mates took it downstream to the old bridge, borrowed some pint pots from the nearby Maltsters Arms and had a rare old time, much to the chagrin of the temperance workers.

As boxing gradually achieved a degree of respectability, a local man was to play a key role in ensuring it would be properly recorded. The trade paper, *Boxing News*, was founded in 1909 by press baron Viscount Camrose, born 30 years earlier in Merthyr as plain William Berry.

In later years two more of Tydfil's sons, Ken Jones, of both *Mirrors* and the *Independent*, and John Lloyd, of the *Daily Express*, covered the sport from ringsides around the world.

Jack Jones, a star at home and in Australia

Some of the talent who flocked to Pontypridd's Greenmeadow gym in 1919: Back, from left: Jack Davies, Arthur Heke, Wyndham Williams; Front: Teddy Ryan, Frank Moody, Francis Rossi, Arthur Bishop and Billy Hampton

Former Swansea footballer Ken, of course, was a brother of Spurs and Wales star Cliff, and boxing, too, has often been a family business, with numerous siblings having parallel careers in the ring. Few, however, actually fought each other. The Cross boys from Merthyr did, in 1930. There was no suggestion of a nice, gentle sparring session, either: Dai was disqualified for hitting Fred below the belt.

Many of the area's fighters turned out for local rugby or football teams, but some indulged in other sports. One such was Arthur Eyles, from Dowlais, a noted wrestler with a flair for showmanship, who was good enough with his fists to hold future British bantam champion Bill Beynon to a draw.

Modern superstar Manny Pacquiao is not the first boxer to turn to politics. More than 20 years before Eddie Thomas was elected Mayor of Merthyr, the way had been paved by Penydarren product Gerry Donovan. Another ex-pro, Alby Davies, has worn the mayoral chain of Rhondda Cynon Taff.

Former schoolboy champion Stan Thomas, born in the Pelican pub in Dowlais, whose successful business meant he became universally known as

Alby Davies and Gerry Donovan – two Welsh schoolboy champions who went on to become mayors

'Stan the Pies', chaired the Welsh Area Council from 1977 until 1980. His charity work earned him an MBE and the Freedom of the Borough alongside namesake Eddie.

A Cefn Coed product, referee, choral conductor and boxing historian Wynford Jones, is the current president of the Welsh Ex-Boxers' Association, a role once filled by fellow-townsman Winstone, whose old friend and spar-mate, Don James, has served since 1997 as the organisation's secretary.

And the story is far from over, although the future may look rather different from the past. Lynsey Holdaway, from Abercanaid, reached the quarter-finals of the 2010 women's world championships.

BIBLIOGRAPHY

The following are among many publications consulted during the writing of this book:

Sporting Life, Mirror of Life, Boxing, Boxing News, Boxing Monthly, Western Mail, South Wales Echo, South Wales Daily News, Merthyr Express, Aberdare Leader, Pontypridd Observer.

Class of the 60s, by Wynford Jones (Wynford Jones)

Wales and its Boxers, ed. Peter Stead and Gareth Williams (University of Wales Press)

Occupation Prizefighter: the Freddie Welsh Story, by Andrew Gallimore (Seren)

The Big If: the Life and Death of Johnny Owen, by Rick Broadbent (Macmillan)

A Bagful of Monkeys, by George M. Evans (Carreg Gwalch)

Street Warrior, by Malcolm Price with Stephen Richards (John Blake)

Valley Lives, Book 2: Champions, by Peter Rogers and C. Jacob (Merthyr Library)

Merthyr's Past Pugilists, by Peter Rogers (Peter Rogers)

Cuthbert Taylor: Just a Little Bit Brown, by Peter Rogers (Peter Rogers)

All in my Corner, by Tony Lee (TL Associates)

The following websites were also of use:

Boxrec, Old Merthyr, Welsh Warriors, Amateur Boxing Results, Rootschat, Rootsweb, Ancestry, Find The Past.